W9-BRB-322

Sunset

Ground Covers

The contents of this book are also published as part of the Sunset book
LAWNS & GROUND COVERS

By the Editors of Sunset Books and Sunset Magazine

Common thrift (Armeria maritima)—*a colorful choice for a small space.*

Sunset Publishing Corporation ■ **Menlo Park, California**

The Garden Problem Solver

The wide world of ground covers holds a diverse assortment of truly useful plants. Whether the challenge is topography, water supply, lack of maintenance time, or simply a matter of aesthetics, you're sure to find at least a handful of these garden workhorses that will address your needs perfectly.

This book will acquaint you with fundamental information on soils, planting techniques, and watering guidelines and systems options. Alphabetically arranged plant descriptions profile more than 125 widely grown ground covers and outline their cultural needs, while the easy-reference "Ground Covers at Work" lists help guide your choices in five different categories. Armed with this knowledge, you'll be able to select appealing plants that will be well-matched to your own garden situation, to your climate, and to the amount and kind of maintenance you're able to give.

We extend our thanks to Marianne Lipanovich for assistance with photography, JoAnn Masaoka Van Atta for styling some of the photographs, and to Rik Olson for the map.

Book Editor
Fran Feldman

Research & Text
Philip Edinger

Coordinating Editor
Deborah Thomas Kramer

Design
Joe di Chiarro

Illustrations
Jane McCreary

Photographers
William Aplin: 17 left; **Derek Fell:** 5, 7 top left, 8 top, 10 bottom, 12 bottom, 13, 15, 18, 41, 57, 58, 63, 64, 65, 67, 75, 78, 79; **Gerald R. Fredrick:** 47, 61,68; **Saxon Holt:** 9 top, 10 top, 11, 30, 74; **Horticultural Photography:** 1; **Stephen Marley:** 35, 36, 72; **Ells Marugg:** 9 bottom left and right, 17 right, 37, 38, 39, 42, 46, 51, 55, 66, 69, 76, 77; **Norman A. Plate:** 8 bottom, 14 top; **Bill Ross:** 7 top right, 16 bottom, 56; **Chad Slattery:** 49; **Michael S. Thompson:** 16 top, 33, 34, 43, 44, 48, 50, 53, 54, 59, 62, 71, 73; **Darrow M. Watt:** 6; **Russ Widstrand:** 40; **Tom Wyatt:** 3, 12 top, 14 bottom, 24, 26, 60, 70.

Cover: Nestled amid rocks, a potpourri of ground covers creates handsome mosaic of colors, shapes, and textures. Among this assemblage are common thrift, rupturewort, woolly and creeping thymes, Irish moss, lavender cotton, crane's bill, juniper, and saxifrage. Landscape designer: Konrad Gauder of Landsculpture. Cover design by Susan Bryant. Photography by Saxon Holt.

Editor, Sunset Books: Elizabeth L. Hogan

First printing August 1991

Contents

Blue star creeper (Laurentia fluviatilis) *is true to its name,
growing close to the ground and featuring light blue, star-shaped blossoms.*

Ground Covers

Among the plants referred to as "ground cover" are plants so varied and so capable of thriving in diverse situations and climates that to describe them as versatile is an understatement. What they have in common is relatively low, dense growth, although ground covers range from prostrate woody shrubs to vines, and from spreading perennials to a few that are popularly thought of as bulbs.

Within the rich assortment of ground covers you can find plants that will stand in for lawn; but you'll encounter a far greater number that will prosper in lawn-defeating situations or where lawn maintenance would be an ongoing headache. Ground covers are the obvious solution to such less-than-perfect situations as deep shade, dry or poor soil, hot and dry expanses, steep slopes, and soil infiltrated by competing tree roots. And where water conservation is essential, certain ground covers are the only viable means of achieving an expanse of low verdure.

Colorful tapestry in harmonious shades combines several varieties of moss pink (Phlox subulata).

Ground Covers
at Work

Color through the Seasons

Many ground covers add spice to their utilitarian lives with a display
of colorful flowers, some flamboyant, others restrained.

Dalmatian bellflower (*Campanula portenschlagiana*)
*unrolls its colorful purple carpet in spring and
remains in bloom throughout summer.*

Assertive color of this sunrose (Helianthemum nummularium) *is accurately captured in its variety name 'Fire Dragon'. White, shades of pink, copper, orange, and yellow are other available colors; foliage may be dark green or nearly gray.*

Bountiful in summer, gazanias offer blossoms in shades of yellow and orange, as well as bronze, red, pink, cream, and white.

Ground Covers for Seasonal Color

PLANT	SPRING	SUMMER	FALL	WINTER	ZONES
Achillea		■	■		4–10
Agapanthus		■			9–10
Ajuga reptans	■	■			4–10
Arabis caucasica	■				6–9
Arctostaphylos				■	Vary
Arctotheca calendula	■	■	■	■	9–10
Arenaria balearica	■	■			6–10
Armeria maritima	■				3–10
Bergenia	■			■	3–10
Bougainvillea	■	■			10
Calluna vulgaris			■		5–9
Campanula		■			4–10
Carissa macrocarpa	■	■	■		9–10
Ceanothus	■				8–10
Cerastium tomentosum	■	■			3–10
Ceratostigma plumbaginoides		■	■		6–10
Chamaemelum nobile		■			3–10
Cistus salviifolius	■				8–10
Convallaria majalis	■				3–9
Convolvulus mauritanicus	■	■	■		8–10
Correa pulchella	■		■	■	9–10
Cotoneaster	■		■		Vary
Cotula squalida		■			6–10
Cytisus kewensis	■				6–8
Dalea greggii	■	■			9–10
Dampiera diversifolia	■	■			9–10
Epimedium	■				3–9
Erica	■	■	■	■	Vary
Erigeron karvinskianus	■	■	■		9–10
Erodium chamaedryoides	■	■	■		8–10
Galax urceolata		■			3–8
Gardenia jasminoides 'Radicans'		■			8–10
Gazania	■	■			9–10
Gelsemium sempervirens	■		■		8–10
Genista	■				6–9
Geranium	■	■	■		Vary
Grevillea	■	■			9–10
Hebe		■			Vary
Helianthemum nummularium	■	■			5–10
Helleborus	■			■	Vary

PLANT	SPRING	SUMMER	FALL	WINTER	ZONES
Hemerocallis	■	■	■		3–10
Hippocrepis comosa	■				9–10
Hosta	■	■			3–9
Hypericum calycinum	■	■			6–10
Iberis sempervirens	■				4–10
Ice plant	■	■			Vary
Jasminum polyanthum	■	■			8–10
Lantana	■	■			9–10
Laurentia fluviatilis	■	■			8–10
Liriope		■			Vary
Lonicera	■	■			5–10
Lotus berthelotii	■	■			9–10
Lysimachia nummularia		■			3–10
Mahonia	■				5–9
Mazus reptans	■	■			4–10
Myosotis scorpioides	■	■			4–10
Nepeta faassenii	■	■			4–10
Osteospermum fruticosum	■	■	■	■	9–10
Pelargonium peltatum	■	■	■		9–10
Phlox subulata	■	■			4–9
Polygonum	■	■			Vary
Potentilla	■	■			4–9
Pratia angulata	■	■			7–10
Pyracantha	■		■		Vary
Ranunculus repens 'Pleniflorus'	■				4–9
Rosa	■	■	■		Vary
Rosmarinus officinalis	■		■	■	7–10
Santolina	■				7–10
Saxifraga stolonifera	■				9–10
Scaevola 'Mauve Clusters'	■	■	■		9–10
Sedum	■	■			Vary
Stachys byzantina		■			4–10
Teucrium chamaedrys		■			6–10
Thymus	■	■			4–10
Trachelospermum jasminoides		■			9–10
Vancouveria planipetala	■				7–9
Verbena	■	■	■		Vary
Veronica	■	■			6–10
Vinca	■				Vary
Viola	■	■			Vary
Wedelia trilobata	■	■	■		9–10

Water-thrifty Ground Covers

When water is limited, you can use drought-tolerant ground covers in all garden situations.

Spartan Genista lydia takes little water and poor soil in stride, furnishing an annual display of golden blossoms regardless of conditions.

Vivid and unthirsty duo provides reliable display with little care. Gaudy red and pink flowers are trailing ice plant (Lampranthus spectabilis), highlighted by yellow blossoms of gazania.

*Sparkling, **true blue shades** are hallmark of wild lilacs (Ceanothus); C. griseus horizontalis is a favorite ground cover species.*

Drought-tolerant Ground Covers

PLANT	ZONES
Achillea	4–10
Arctotheca calendula	9–10
Artemisia caucasica	5–9
Atriplex semibaccata	8–10
Baccharis pilularis	8–10
Ceanothus	8–10
Cistus salviifolius	9–10
Cotoneaster	Vary
Dalea greggii	9–10
Erigeron karvinskianus	9–10
Festuca ovina glauca	3–10
Genista	6–9
Grevillea	9–10
Hypericum calycinum	6–10
Ice plant (some)	Vary
Juniperus	Vary
Lantana	9–10
Mahonia	Vary
Polygonum cuspidatum compactum	4–10
Ribes viburnifolium	9–10
Rosmarinus officinalis	7–10
Santolina	7–10
Scaevola 'Mauve Clusters'	9–10
Teucrium chamaedrys	6–10

*Rugged, **adaptable Aaron's beard** (Hypericum calycinum), at left and above, performs in sun or shade, with either little or regular garden watering.*

...Water-thrifty Ground Covers

Reliable, undemanding junipers—
this one is Juniperus chinensis procumbens—
are valued for their unchanging good
appearance year-round.

Molten shades transform rock cotoneaster (*Cotoneaster horizontalis*) each fall before leaves drop. Little water often results in a more colorful foliage display.

A Preference for Shade

The coolness and reduced light intensity of shade offer preferred conditions for many ground covers.

Shaggy turf of mondo grass (Ophiopogon japonicus) gives a solid, grassy effect in shaded locations where real grasses languish.

Silvery gray leaves of Lamium maculatum 'Beacon Silver' (at right) brighten shady gardens throughout growing season.

...A Preference for Shade

Versatile English ivy (Hedera helix) provides a lush, neat carpet of foliage year-round in exposures ranging from full sun to heavy shade.

Shade-tolerant Ground Covers

PLANT	ZONES
Aegopodium podagraria	4–8
Ajuga reptans	4–10
Ardisia japonica	8–9
Asarum caudatum	5–9
Cornus canadensis	3–6
Duchesnea indica	3–10
Epimedium	3–9
Euonymus fortunei	5–9
Galax urceolata	3–8
Galium odoratum	5–10
Gaultheria	Vary
Hedera	Vary
Helleborus	Vary
Herniaria glabra	5–10
Hosta	3–9
Houttuynia cordata	6–10
Hypericum calycinum	6–10
Lamium maculatum	5–10
Liriope	Vary
Mahonia nervosa	5–9
Myosotis scorpioides	4–10
Ophiopogon japonicus	8–10
Pachysandra terminalis	4–9
Paxistima	5–9
Ranunculus repens 'Pleniflorus'	4–9
Rubus calycinoides	7–9
Sarcococca hookerana humilis	6–10
Saxifraga stolonifera	9–10
Soleirolia soleirolii	9–10
Taxus baccata 'Repandens'	6–10
Vancouveria planipetala	7–9
Viburnum davidii	7–10
Vinca	Vary
Viola	Vary
Wedelia trilobata	9–10

Touches of white in foliage of variegated Bishop's weed (Aegopodium podagraria 'Variegatum') sparkle in sun or shade.

Hostas and shade *are natural companions. Leaf colors, sizes, and shapes vary widely; this sea of greens is 'Frances Williams'.*

Legendary fragrance *emanates from violets (Viola odorata), which come in shades of blue, lavender, violet, pink, and white, as well as traditional purple.*

Plants for "*Living Carpets*"

Ground-hugging plants offer the neatness and uniformity of turf grass without the lawn's need for frequent maintenance.

*Acting as "**living mortar**," Irish moss (Sagina subulata) unites paving and rock outcrop with border of colorful annuals. Occasional footsteps leave it undamaged.*

Stepping-stones float *in a pool of blue star creeper (Laurentia fluviatilis); planting accepts moderate foot traffic.*

Undemanding goldmoss sedum (Sedum acre) spreads springtime haze of yellow flowers over foliage cover of light green, fleshy leaves.

Low-growing Ground Covers

PLANT	ZONES	PLANT	ZONES
Ajuga reptans	4–10	*Phyla nodiflora	9–10
Arabis caucasica	6–9	Polygonum capitatum	9–10
*Arenaria balearica	6–10	*Potentilla	4–9
*Chamaemelum nobile	3–10	Pratia angulata	7–10
Cotula squalida	6–10	*Sagina subulata	5–10
Dampiera diversifolia	9–10	Saxifraga stolonifera	9–10
*Duchesnea indica	3–10	Scaevola 'Mauve Clusters'	9–10
*Erodium chamaedryoides	8–10	Sedum	Vary
Euonymus fortunei 'Minima'	5–9	Soleirolia soleirolii	9–10
Helianthemum nummularium	5–10	Stachys byzantina 'Silver Carpet'	4–10
*Herniara glabra	5–10	Teucrium chamaedrys 'Prostrata'	6–10
*Hippocrepis comosa	9–10	Thymus praecox arcticus	4–10
Ice plant (some)	Vary	Verbena	Vary
Lamium maculatum	5–10	Veronica repens	6–10
*Laurentia fluviatilis	8–10	Vinca minor	4–10
*Lotus	Vary	Viola	Vary
Lysimachia nummularia	3–10	Waldsteinia fragarioides	5–10
*Mazus reptans	4–10	*Zoysia tenuifolia	9–10
*Mentha requienii	7–10		

*Tolerates some foot traffic

Choices for Hillsides

Natural problem solvers, ground covers thrive on sloping sites that are hard to water, have shallow soil, or are exposed to harsh winds.

Two foolproof ground covers—*juniper (Juniperus) and ivy (Hedera)—combine to cloak sloping ground with solid foliage cover. Roots of each help control erosion.*

Ivy geranium *(Pelargonium peltatum) is a warm-weather favorite for blanketing slopes with year-round color.*

Warm-climate classic for hillside cover is trailing ice plant (Lampranthus spectabilis). Gray green, fingerlike foliage is concealed beneath fluorescent flowers.

Combined planting of heath (Erica) and Scotch heather (Calluna vulgaris) creates tumbling froth of foliage and flower colors.

Ground Covers for Hillsides

PLANT	ZONES	PLANT	ZONES
Arctostaphylos	Vary	Hemerocallis	3–10
Arctotheca calendula	9–10	*Hippocrepis comosa	9–10
*Arundinaria pygmaea	7–10	*Hypericum calycinum	6–10
Atriplex semibaccata	8–10	Ice plant (many)	Vary
Baccharis pilularis	8–10	*Juniperus	Vary
Bougainvillea	10	*Lantana	9–10
Calluna vulgaris	5–9	*Lonicera	5–10
Carissa macrocarpa	9–10	*Lotus corniculatus	5–10
*Ceanothus	8–10	*Mahonia	5–9
*Cissus	9–10	*Myoporum parvifolium	9–10
*Cistus salviifolius	8–10	Osteospermum fruticosum	9–10
Convolvulus mauritanicus	8–10	Pelargonium peltatum	9–10
Coprosma	9–10	*Polygonum cuspidatum compactum	4–10
*Coronilla varia	3–10	*Pyracantha	Vary
Correa pulchella	9–10	*Ribes viburnifolium	9–10
*Cotoneaster	Vary	Rosa	Vary
Cytisus kewensis	6–8	*Rosmarinus officinalis	7–10
Erica	Vary	Santolina	7–10
*Euonymus fortunei	5–9	Taxus baccata 'Repandens'	6–10
Genista	6–9	*Trachelospermum jasminoides	9–10
Grevillea	9–10	*Vinca	Vary
*Hedera	Vary	Zoysia tenuifolia	9–10

*Helps control erosion

Ground Covers— The Basics

Success with ground covers starts with an assessment of your site: soil character, climate, the sun/shade ratio where you're planting, and the availability of water to the plants. Once you've collected this data, you can begin making your choices (see page 33).

Here we present the information you'll need to plant your ground cover, supply it with water, and care for it.

Design & Planting

Nature abounds in ground covers. Some are obvious—vast sweeps of prostrate manzanita in the mountains or at northern seashores, for example. Others, such as the mixed assortment of ferns, trilliums, and other semishade plants in an open woodland, are less frequently recognized as the ground covers they are.

Yet, to many people, ground covers only come to mind when the lawn is removed and the question arises about what to put in its place.

The Advantages of Ground Covers

Replacing turf grass with ground cover is just one of the practical uses of such plants. Many will, indeed, blanket large, flat expanses of ground while demanding less water and care than a comparable expanse of grass. And, by carefully choosing the appropriate ground cover, you can plant areas where a turf grass would be impractical or simply would not grow well.

Some ground covers will grow eagerly on slopes where a lawn is hard to care for; in addition, the ground cover can help prevent erosion and gullying. In dense shade, in areas where tree roots compete for water and nutrients, and in soils that are regularly too moist or too dry, some ground covers will thrive. Ground-hugging types are natural choices for planting between paving stones and garden steps.

Designing with Ground Covers

Ground covers have an artistic side as well as a practical one. They're particularly well suited for creating landscape patterns. Because ground covers are low and dense, you can spread them over the landscape as if they were brush strokes on a canvas: broad and flowing curves, discreet, geometric patches—whatever is appropriate in the overall design.

In addition, you can create a nearly infinite variety of contrasts and associations—ground cover with lawn, with

Potpourri of ground cover plants lends variety to landscape. Featured prominently are, left center, rock cotoneaster (Cotoneaster horizontalis) and, right center, Scotch heather (Calluna vulgaris).

other ground covers, with shrubs and vines, and with annuals and perennials.

Color and texture offer additional design choices. Foliage textures range from grassy to tropically bold; color encompasses subtle gray shades, soft to glossy green, bronze to purple, and variegated combinations of green to gray with yellow to white. And many ground cover plants provide some type of seasonal flower color— sometimes showy fruits as well.

Because ground cover plants are low growing, they can be used to create variety in the landscape without contributing bulk that would seem to close in on the space. Unlike turf grass, ground covers don't invite you to walk across them (although some can take limited foot traffic), so they can function as traffic barriers while offering no barrier to sight.

Soil Basics

Successful gardening—be it ground covers, vegetables, or roses—starts with an understanding of your garden's soil. Knowing the characteristics of your soil will influence your choice of plants, your approach to soil preparation, and your watering practices—how you apply water and how frequently you do it.

Soil Types

Soil is a dynamic relationship between soil particles, air, water, and organic matter. Initially, the nature of the soil particles—their sizes, shapes, and relative quantities—determines a soil's type and governs the air/water relationship within the soil. Organic matter enhances a soil's quality, affecting permeability (both of water and roots), drainage, and, to some extent, nutrient potential.

Clay and sand, the smallest and largest of the mineral particles in soil, give their names to two soil types. When both clay and sand particles are present along with silt, an intermediate-size particle, the soil is called loam. In reality, most soils fall somewhere in between those three types. You'll have to determine which one your soil most closely resembles.

Clay soil contains the smallest particles, each of which is flattened so that they fit closely together with little space between them for air and water (see illustration below). This is the "heavy" or "adobe" soil that's sticky when wet and cracks when dry. Squeeze a handful of wet clay soil and it will stay in a lump, the excess oozing between your fingers.

Water percolates slowly through clay, so this soil is considered poorly drained. But this slowness also means that it retains moisture the longest and thus can go without watering for greater lengths of time than other soil types. Dissolved nutrients also remain longer in clay.

Sandy soil is the opposite of clay. Particles are distinctly larger (up to 250 times the size of clay particles); because they're rounded rather than flat, they group together more loosely, with relatively large spaces between particles. Sandy soil feels gritty rather than sticky; squeeze a handful of wet sandy soil and it will fall apart when you release your grip or give it a slight prod.

Drainage in sandy soil is excellent, but water retention is poor; dissolved nutrients also leach away fairly rapidly.

For this reason, plants in sand need watering and fertilizing more often than those in clay.

Loam, touted as the ideal garden soil, contains both clay and sand particles as well as silt particles, considered intermediate in character between the two extremes; organic matter also is a component of loam.

This soil drains well but not too rapidly, so moisture retention is good. It leaches nutrients only moderately and contains enough air for healthy root growth.

Many gardens have soil that deviates from the "ideal" loam, but this is not a cause for despair. Many popular plants will prosper in a range of soils tending toward either extreme. Also, you can improve your soil by adding amendments when you prepare it for planting, as discussed on the facing page.

Acid or Alkaline Soil

Independent of soil type, soil may be acid, neutral, or alkaline; this is expressed in the pH scale that runs from 1 (extremely acid) to 14 (extremely alkaline), with 7 as the neutral point.

Soil Particles & Types

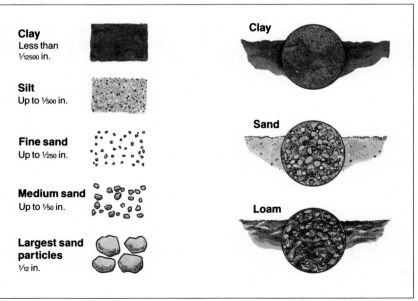

Clay
Less than 1/12500 in.

Silt
Up to 1/500 in.

Fine sand
Up to 1/250 in.

Medium sand
Up to 1/50 in.

Largest sand particles
1/12 in.

Clay

Sand

Loam

The majority of popular garden plants will thrive in soils that are moderately acid (about pH 6.5) to slightly alkaline (around pH 7.1); at higher and lower readings, certain nutrients may become unavailable to plants, thereby hindering growth. But some plants do have fairly specific pH needs, usually for acid soil (those that do are noted in the descriptions beginning on page 33).

A soil test will quickly reveal the acidity or alkalinity of your soil. Simple test kits, good enough to give you a close reading, are sold at nurseries and garden centers; professional soil laboratories can run more precise tests.

If your soil tests either highly acid or alkaline, check with your local County Cooperative Extension agent for advice on treatment appropriate for your region.

Preparing the Soil

Readying the soil for planting entails several steps, as outlined below.

Step 1: Weeding. Weeds—the bane of a gardener's existence—can easily spoil the appearance of a uniform ground cover. But weeds don't have to be a fact of your gardening life if you attend to some careful preparation.

Thoroughly clear all weeds from the area you intend to plant. A sharp hoe will dispatch shallow-rooted weeds easily. For the deep-rooted, perennial sorts (such as dandelions and Bermuda grass), you'll have to dig them out by hand to be sure of total control; make sure to pull out the weeds' roots as well as their tops.

If hoeing or hand-pulling is too daunting, you can rotary-till the ground and then rake out the dislodged weeds. Use this method only if annual weeds are the problem; tilling can actually help the spread of perennial weeds.

For thorough control of most annual and perennial weeds with minimum effort, you can spray the weeds with the systemic herbicide glyphosate and then prepare the soil after the weeds have been killed. Be sure to follow label directions to the letter and avoid getting herbicide on any desirable plants.

Step 2: Digging the soil. Dig or till the area to be planted—if the ground is level or only slightly sloping—to remove any foreign matter, such as rocks, roots, or buried construction debris. On distinctly sloping sites, it's better to leave the soil surface as undisturbed as possible so that erosion potential is minimized.

Step 3: Grading. Grade relatively level sites, if necessary, to eliminate humps and fill in hollows. A rake (either bow or level-head) should do the job.

Step 4: Adding amendments. Amend the soil (in level or gently sloping sites) with organic matter (see below) and any material needed to alter the pH. This is also the time to add phosphorus and potassium fertilizer to the soil, as these two nutrients are not readily soluble and must be dug into the soil where roots will take hold.

Spade or till all amendments and fertilizers into the soil to a depth of about 9 inches, rake the soil smooth, and water it. If low spots show up after watering, fill them in before you plant.

Using Organic Amendments

The decay of organic matter is part of a natural cycle that continually improves soil. Microorganisms break down plant and animal remains that fall to the soil or are dug into it; during the process, the bits of organic matter lodge between soil particles.

In clay soil, the decaying matter wedges between particles and groups of particles, opening up the soil so that water, air, and roots can penetrate more easily. In sand, the organic matter lodges in the relatively large spaces between particles, slowing the passage of water through the soil and rendering it more retentive of water and important nutrients.

Eventually, organic matter is completely reduced by soil microorganisms, depriving a soil of its benefits unless new material is added. With permanent plantings, you can't dig more organic matter into the root area, but an organic mulch (see page 27) will provide material for continued breakdown so that the upper portion of the soil will remain permeable.

Materials to use. Nurseries and garden centers routinely sell packaged organic materials such as peat moss, nitrogen-fortified wood products, and animal manures.

To calculate your needs, remember that a standard 2¼-cubic-foot bag will give a 3-inch layer over 9 square feet of soil. You may also be able to buy some materials—especially wood products and various by-products of regional agriculture—in bulk.

How to add organic amendments. The best way to add organic matter when planting is to dig it into the entire area you intend to plant.

Spread the organic matter over the soil and dig or till it in; use a quarter to a third the volume of organic matter to soil volume—for example, dig a 2-inch layer of organic matter into 6 to 8 inches of soil.

If you're planting ground covers from large (1- or 2-gallon) containers, you can simply add organic matter to the soil you return to the planting hole, providing your soil is sandy to sandy loam.

In heavier soils, however, organically amended backfill soil absorbs water more quickly than the surrounding soil can absorb it; the result can be plant death from waterlogged roots. In such soils, return the native soil to the planting hole; an organic mulch spread over the ground will help improve the top few inches in time.

Three Planting Methods for Ground Covers

To plant small plants from pots, packs, or flats, *dig a hole just deep enough for root ball. Top of ball should be even with surface.*

To plant from a 1- or 2-gallon container, *taper hole outward, creating a plateau for root ball. Top of ball should be slightly above grade.*

On a steep slope, *set a plant from a 1- or 2-gallon container on its own terrace with top of root ball high; dig a watering basin behind plant.*

Planting Techniques

You'll find plants for ground cover sold in several different ways. The spreading, root-as-they-go types such as ivy (*Hedera*) may be available in flats that contain numerous individual plants. Some perennial ground covers can be bought in packs (four, six, or eight plants in individual root balls) or in small pots. Many woody ground covers come in containers of 1- or 2-gallon size.

The illustrations above show planting methods for ground covers.

When to Plant

The best time of year to plant a ground cover is when it will have the longest possible time to become established before being stressed by unfavorable weather. In mild-winter regions, fall and winter are the best planting seasons: they allow root growth during the cool part of the year so the plants will be ready to grow vigorously at the onset of warm weather.

Gardeners in low- and intermediate-elevation deserts will want to plant just as soon as cool weather sets in. In cold-winter regions where snow can be expected and soil routinely freezes, plant in early spring just after the soil can be worked.

Summer—except in cool-summer areas—is the least desirable planting time. Plants are slower to establish when stressed by heat, and they need close attention to watering to forestall wilting.

Spacing Plants

The best planting distance between plants depends on the particular ground cover and, to some extent, on how quickly you want the area blanketed with growth.

The individual plant descriptions beginning on page 33 contain guidelines for spacing the plants. The chart below shows you how to calculate the amount of ground that will be covered by specified numbers of plants at various spacings between plants.

Watering

Some water is essential to the growth of any plant, even one that's drought tolerant. It follows, then, that you'll need to know how to satisfy your plants' water needs. And, in the process, you'll want to choose from among the several options available for supplying water to your ground cover plantings, as explained in the following sections.

Watering Guidelines

All ground covers need some watering at some time. But not all will need the same amount of water each time, nor

Spacing between Plants	Area Plants Will Cover			
	48 plants	64 plants	72 plants	100 plants
6 in.	10 sq. ft.	13½ sq. ft.	15½ sq. ft.	21½ sq. ft.
8 in.	18 sq. ft.	24½ sq. ft.	27½ sq. ft.	38 sq. ft.
10 in.	28½ sq. ft.	38½ sq. ft.	43 sq. ft.	60 sq. ft.
12 in.	41½ sq. ft.	55½ sq. ft.	62½ sq. ft.	86½ sq. ft.
15 in.	64½ sq. ft.	86 sq. ft.	97 sq. ft.	135 sq. ft.
18 in.	92 sq. ft.	123 sq. ft.	138 sq. ft.	192 sq. ft.
24 in.	165½ sq. ft.	220½ sq. ft.	248 sq. ft.	344½ sq. ft.

will they all need watering at the same time intervals.

The water requirements of each ground cover depend on a number of factors, including soil conditions, climate, and depth of roots. For information on the needs of each type, see the descriptions beginning on page 33.

How Much, How Often?

If you know your soil type and its characteristics (see page 20), you'll understand how water behaves when it contacts your soil. You'll be able to judge the rate of penetration (slow in clay, rapid in sand) and then estimate the amount of water you'll need to apply to gain the required penetration.

How often you should water depends first on your ground cover: does it need regular moisture or just infrequent watering? Your soil also influences intervals between watering; clay soil retains moisture the longest, sand the shortest.

Finally, climate and time of year affect the length of time a soil remains moist. Cool, moist climates (and times of year) stretch intervals between waterings; hot regions (and summers) impose greater frequencies.

Water Delivery Systems

For virtually all ground cover situations, there are two basic methods for applying water. One is to use a sprinkler head attached to the end of a hose; you place the sprinkler every time you water. The other is to use a water system with stationary points of water emission—an underground sprinkler system or a drip-irrigation system.

Hose-end sprinkling. With this watering method, you can choose from a wide array of sprinklers with differing modes of dispersing water. Sprinklers can be handy if one or two placements will cover all your ground cover. More than that, however, and moving the sprinkler becomes a nuisance. You also must be sure to overlap areas for even application to all parts of your planting.

Water waste is the inherent drawback to any hose-end sprinkler. Spray thrown into the air is subject to evaporation and wind drift; the volume of water delivered often is greater than soil can absorb easily, resulting in puddling and runoff after a short period of time, especially in heavier soils; and, if the sprinkler isn't carefully positioned, you can wastefully water paved surfaces along with your plants.

Stationary watering systems. If you want to set up a water delivery system with fixed-position watering heads, you have a choice between two types. One is the rigid-pipe, in-ground system with sprinkler heads— traditionally used for watering lawns. The more recent innovation is the drip-irrigation system, which features flexible plastic tubing laid on or just under the surface of the soil.

Because drip systems can be easily tailored to watering expanses of ground cover, detailed instructions for assembly are given, beginning on page 25.

Underground Sprinkler Systems

Some gardeners prefer a rigid-pipe underground system with fixed sprinkler heads for watering high, shrubby ground covers (some *Cotoneaster* species, for example) and those covers that form a solid mass of roots from countless plants, such as *Hypericum*. Risers elevate sprinkler heads just above the foliage; the spray of water moistens all the soil beneath.

Components of an underground system. Following are the basic components of such a system.

■ *Rigid polyvinyl chloride (PVC) pipe,* much easier to install and longer lasting than traditional galvanized pipe, is now the material of choice for underground watering systems. Pipes, which come in 10- or 20-foot lengths, are cut to length with pipe cutters or a hacksaw and are easily joined to each other or to special fittings with solvent.

■ *Sprinkler heads on risers* are positioned so that coverage overlaps and an even amount of water is distributed over the entire area.

You can choose from a variety of sprinkler heads; select the type that suits the shape of the area to be covered. Heads that produce a fountain of spray (or a partial fountain) water narrow plantings well; they also can be laid out in a grid pattern to cover large expanses.

If you'll be combining full- and partial-circle heads, look for matched-precipitation-rate heads that emit proportionate volumes (a head producing a 90° fan of spray delivers a quarter the amount of water of a full-circle head).

To minimize runoff potential, try low-precipitation-rate heads; these deliver water at a slower rate than normal heads.

For larger expanses of ground cover, good sprinkler choices are impact sprinklers and single-stream or multistream rotor types. These throw water a distance of 40 feet or more (depending on the model), so you need fewer heads. Most of these impact and rotor sprinklers have slow application rates (check the different models for precipitation rates) that allow the soil to absorb water with a minimum of runoff.

■ *Control valves equipped with antisiphon devices,* either integral or separate, operate circuits, each designed to serve plants with similar water needs.

■ *A manifold,* or a grouping of control valves, simplifies the operation of a multicircuit underground system and allows it to be operated automatically, if desired, when wired to a controller, or timer (see below).

■ *A controller,* the heart of an automatic system, can be programmed to turn each circuit on and off (for a description, see page 25).

Designing and installing a system. Manufacturers of underground sprinkler systems provide detailed instructions on designing and installing a system; look for their workbooks where irrigation equipment is sold. Pipes must be buried underground in trenches.

Although installing a system isn't difficult, digging trenches, laying pipes, and attaching the other equipment can take several days. If you prefer to hire a professional rather than do the work yourself, ask friends or neighbors for references. Or look in the Yellow Pages under "Irrigation Systems & Equipment," "Landscape Contractors," or "Sprinklers—Garden & Lawn."

Drip Irrigation

Many gardeners, particularly those living in regions where water conservation is paramount, prefer to water ground covers with some sort of drip-irrigation setup.

Unlike an in-ground sprinkler system, which uses high water pressure and volume to dispense water over a large area, drip irrigation delivers water at low pressure and volume to specific areas—often to individual plants; penetration is slow, its depth regulated by the length of time the system is on.

The result is well-watered plants with less use of water than with sprinklers. Drip emitters, which release water directly to the soil, waste virtually no water; even mini-sprays and mini-sprinklers, which spray water into the air, conserve much more water than ordinary sprinklers. The system can be connected to your water line or operated from a hose bibb or the end of a hose.

Look for drip-irrigation materials and fittings at irrigation supply stores.

Basic Components

A drip-irrigation system is easy to assemble and can be modified when your needs change. Most systems are made from polyvinyl tubing fitted with emitters or sprays. The components of a typical system are shown in the photograph above.

Tubing. The standard way to distribute water is through 1/2- or 3/8-inch flexible black poly tubing attached with plastic fittings and laid on the surface of the soil, where it can be obscured by a mulch

Components of a Drip-irrigation System

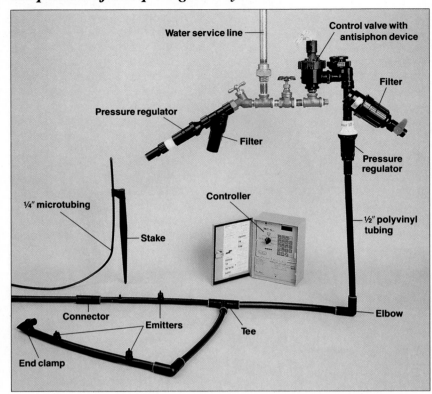

(see page 27) or by foliage. (For a sturdier but less flexible system, you can use PVC pipe for main lines and poly tubing for lateral lines.)

Thin, 1/4-inch microtubing, often referred to as "spaghetti tubing," can run from the main line to individual plants.

Emitters and sprayers. You can choose from a variety of emitters, all of which deliver water through small openings at low flow rates. They're fitted directly into the main tubing or into the ends of microtubing. Add to these a choice of mini-sprayers and mini-sprinklers (see at right), and you have great latitude in design.

■ *Drip emitters* are best for watering individual plants, such as shrubby ground covers. Water placement is more precise than with mini-sprayers or mini-sprinklers, and the emitters can be completely hidden from view.

Some drip emitters are pressure-compensating, providing a steady flow

rate despite low or high pressure from the tap. Use these emitters if your setup spans an elevation change greater than 10 feet, if lateral lines exceed 200 feet, or if emitters on a line add up to more than 100 gallons per hour (gph).

■ *Mini-sprayers and mini-sprinklers* spread water over a wider area than drip emitters, but they still operate at low flow rates and low pressure. They're better for closely spaced perennial ground covers and those that root along spreading stems. You can also use them to water higher-growing, shrubby ground covers if you extend them above the foliage (drip emitters at ground level will give more efficient penetration with less waste, however).

Mini-sprayers are available in various spray patterns—from full circle to a fraction of a circle—so you can use them in tight or irregularly shaped spaces. The radius of coverage ranges from 4 to 10 feet; water output varies from 3 to 30 gph.

Mini-sprinklers emit larger droplets than mini-sprayers, so they're less affected by wind. All give full-circle coverage (with radii from 10 to 30 feet) at outputs ranging from 3 to 30 gph.

Valves. You'll need a valve that will turn the water on and off. If you design a hose-end system, you'll use the hose bibb. But if you connect directly to your water line, you'll need a valve with an antisiphon backflow preventer; the two come separately or as an integral unit.

Filter. Particulate impurities in water are the Achilles heel of drip systems; a good filter (installed just below the antisiphon device) will save you the time and frustration of cleaning clogged emitters.

A Y-filter with 150- to 200-mesh fiberglass or stainless steel screen is best for systems connected directly to a water source. For hose-bibb or hose-end systems, connect an in-line filter directly to the hose bibb; then add a pressure regulator (see below) and attach the system's main feeder line to it or to the end of a hose that connects between the pressure regulator and the drip system.

Pressure regulator. The components of a low-volume system are designed to operate best at water pressures between 20 and 30 pounds per square inch (psi). However, many household water lines operate at higher pressures. (To find out what your water pressure is, call your water department; or buy or borrow a gauge to measure pressure at the faucet. If your water pressure is over 75 psi, it's considered high.)

Most drip-irrigation systems need a pressure regulator, installed between the filter and the main drip line, for best performance. Preset to 20 or 30 psi, it reduces the pressure to a rate that the system can accept.

Optional Equipment

Three other devices are available for incorporation into a drip system. One operates the system for you, another expands the system's function, and a third helps you conserve water.

Controller. Popularly referred to as a timer, a controller is an electronic device that automatically regulates the operation of each system connected to it. Multiprogram controllers let you set up different watering frequencies and durations on different lines, so that plants with different water needs receive the right amounts of water—whether or not you're home.

Most new controllers are solid state, making them far more versatile than the older mechanical types. Before you purchase one, be sure that you can operate it easily and that it accommodates the needs of your system.

Fertilizer injector. Particularly useful with drip-irrigation systems, where water is applied directly to the soil, a fertilizer injector will add liquid fertilizer to your watering system.

You have a choice of types. For hose-end drip systems, you can use either a siphon attachment that sucks liquid fertilizer concentrate from a bucket and puts it into the system or a cartridge attachment that holds special dry but soluble fertilizers. Both devices attach between the hose bibb and the filter.

For drip systems connected directly to your household water line, you can install a fertilizer-injector canister in each system between the antisiphon device and the filter. The canister accommodates either liquid fertilizer (not fish emulsion, which can clog emitters) or dissolved dry fertilizer.

Automatic rain shutoff valve. Mounted out in the open, an automatic rain shutoff device measures rainfall and automatically inactivates your system when water reaches a certain level. This interruption of your programmed watering schedule prevents the watering of rain-soaked plantings—or automatic watering during rainfall. When the water evaporates, the system turns back on.

Design & Assembly

Advance planning is crucial to the success of a drip-irrigation system. Such planning includes overall concept, layout of lines, choice of emitters, and number of emitters placed on one line. Be sure you know your soil type, since water moves differently through different soils (see chart below).

Planning your system. Start by sketching the area (or areas) on paper. Pencil in water sources and any obstacles, such as patios or walkways, between the water source and the area to be served. Also mark any slopes or elevation changes—they can affect water distribution.

Next, determine the flow rate of water from your garden faucet. To do this, turn off all water indoors. Then turn on the faucet outdoors and accumulate water in a bucket for 30 seconds. Measure the number of gallons in the bucket and multiply that figure by 120. This will give you the gallons per hour (gph) your water lines will deliver.

Emitter Flow Rate	Amount & Pattern of Coverage		
½ gph 1 gph 2 gph	1 sq. ft. 5 sq. ft. 11 sq. ft.	5 sq. ft. 11 sq. ft. 18 sq. ft.	11 sq. ft. 18 sq. ft. 31 sq. ft.
	Sandy Soil	Loam	Clay Soil

A gallon of drip-irrigated water moves differently through three kinds of soil. Numbers for each give maximum horizontal coverage at different emitter flow rates (expressed in gallons per hour). Shading shows vertical wetting pattern.

From this figure you can calculate the number of emitters you can place on one drip-irrigation line, remembering that the emitters' total output (in gph) should not exceed 75 percent of available water flow at the faucet.

Laying out lines. Group plants on separate valves according to water needs. Be careful not to run lines too long or to put too many emitters on one line: the tubing has limits on how much water it can efficiently handle. Remember: Running a line uphill shortens the possible run, downhill increases it (for information about running lines on slopes, see below, at right).

You can either bury the lines 2 to 3 inches in the soil or leave them on the surface. Buried lines last longer, are less prone to disturbance, and don't affect the appearance of your garden. But lines left on the surface are easier to install, repair, and maintain. By adding a 2-inch layer of mulch over them, you create many of the same benefits that you have with buried lines.

Choosing and spacing emitters. The number and gallonage of emitters you use for each plant will depend on your soil and the plants you're watering.

As a rule of thumb, use higher-gpm emitters for ground covers in sandy soil, lower ones for shallow-rooted plants in clay soil. Also, space drip emitters closer together for shallow-rooted ground covers, such as many perennials and spreading root-along-the-stem kinds. Refer to the chart below for guidelines.

Spacing is greatly affected by the layout of the plants. If plants are spaced

Installation Tools

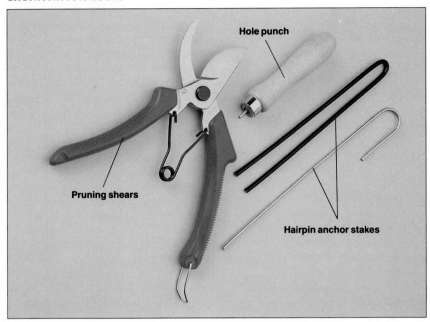

Hole punch

Pruning shears

Hairpin anchor stakes

less than about 2 feet apart in a confined bed, there's no need to design a system to suit each plant.

Systematizing a slope. Gravity slows the flow of water uphill and speeds it downhill. Therefore, if your lines will run on sloping soil, such as a bank or hillside, you'll want to plan to set valves and antisiphon backflow preventers at the top of the slope. Run main lines perpendicular to the slope and lateral lines parallel to it.

If you'll be watering shrubby ground covers with emitters, be sure to use the pressure-compensating kind. If you plan to use mini-sprayers, choose half-circle sprays and position them so they spray downhill.

Installing the system. To assemble a drip system, you'll need some simple tools, shown above: pruning shears to cut tubing, a hole-punching device to install emitters, and a number of hairpin anchor stakes to secure the tubing to the ground.

Following the order shown in the photograph on page 24, assemble the valves, filter, and pressure regulator. If you're connecting your system directly to a water line, place a shutoff valve between your system and the water line; this will allow you to shut off the irriga-

Plants	Soil Type	Number & Size of Emitter
Low shrubs	Sandy soil Loam Clay soil	One 2-gph emitter next to plant One 1-gph emitter next to plant One ½-gph emitter next to plant
Ground covers spaced at least 2 feet apart	Sandy soil or loam Clay soil	One 1-gph emitter at root ball One ½-gph emitter at root ball
Closer ground covers with less distinct root zones	Any soil	Overlapping mini-sprayers or mini-sprinklers
Beds of ground covers	Sandy soil Loam Clay soil	Several 2-gph emitters spaced about a foot apart in a row Several 1-gph emitters spaced about 1½ feet apart in a row Several ½-gph emitters spaced about 1½ feet apart in a row

tion system but still use the faucet. Wrap threaded connections with pipe tape before attaching them. Hand-tighten plastic fittings.

Connect the tubing to the valve assembly and lay out the main distribution lines; whenever possible, place them next to walls and edges of paths where they'll be easy to find and more protected from disturbance. Then attach lateral lines with tee and elbow fittings. Use hairpin stakes to secure all tubing in place.

Try not to get dirt in the system when assembling lines and installing emitters. Flush all lines before you close off the ends.

To punch holes in the tubing for emitters, hold the hole punch perpendicular to the tubing, squeeze the tube on each side with your fingers to keep it from flattening, and then push and twist straight down. Don't take a punch out and try to reinsert it—the hole may get so big it will leak.

If you're installing an automated system, mount the controller in a convenient place and wire the valves to it, following the instructions provided by the manufacturer.

Once the system is assembled, flush the lines again and then turn it on. To confirm that you have enough emitters in the right places, let the system run for its normal cycle, wait several hours, and then dig into the soil in several places to check the spread of moisture. If necessary, add or reposition some of the emitters.

Maintenance

To the gardener who is familiar with taking care of a lawn, the word "maintenance" immediately suggests weekly mowing.

But maintenance for ground covers—mulching, fertilizing, grooming, and controlling any pests or diseases—comes around far less often. In fact, a careful choice of plants can often reduce the need for any maintenance to once a year or less.

Mulches for Ground Covers

An aid to getting any ground cover off to a good start is a mulch over the bare earth between plants. Not only does this benefit the plants, but it also offers attractiveness—the mulch makes a uniform carpet that ties together the new planting.

The Advantages of Mulch

The traditional mulch is a layer of loose-textured organic material, 1 to perhaps 4 inches thick, spread over the soil. This layer retards the loss of surface moisture so the root zone stays moist for a longer period of time after watering. In hot weather, a mulch helps to lower soil temperature beneath its blanket.

These conditions favor good root growth and help plants establish themselves more quickly; eventually, the ground cover itself will form its own living mulch.

In addition, a mulch suppresses weed growth by effectively burying seeds and preventing their germination. Any weeds that do come up in the mulch can be pulled easily because of the mulch's loose texture.

A mulch also helps prevent erosion and gullying: it intercepts the force of rainfall (or watering); water percolates easily through a mulch instead of scouring the bare earth. This is especially important on gently sloping sites. Finally, an organic mulch, as it decomposes, improves the composition of the top few inches of soil.

Materials & Methods

You have a wide choice among potential mulch materials—from coarse to fine textured, and from long lasting to ephemeral. Aside from appearance, deciding factors will be cost and local availability. Whatever you choose, be sure it won't pack down into a sodden mass, repelling water rather than admitting it.

Because a mulch keeps the soil beneath cooler than if unmulched, it's best to delay applying mulch to new plantings until the soil has warmed. If applied early in the year when the soil is still cold, a mulch can slow root growth by keeping the ground too cool.

Here are some of the more generally available materials.

Wood products. Wood products, which include ground bark and sawdust, are sold bagged or in bulk form.

Ground bark may be from fir, pine, hemlock, or redwood; it's long lasting (especially redwood) and attractive, in tones of brown aging to gray. Textures range from fine to 2-inch chips.

Fine-textured sawdust needs nitrogen for its decomposition; otherwise, it will take available nitrogen from the soil for the process. Commercially packaged sawdust usually is nitrogen fortified; raw sawdust requires a nitrogen supplement: ½ pound actual nitrogen for every 100 square feet of mulch spread 1 inch deep.

Straw. Although short-lived and coarse textured, straw is reasonably attractive, inexpensive, and widely available.

Animal manures. Also widely available, manure is sold both commercially packaged and in bulk. As a mulch its effective lifetime is about a year. Apply only aged or composted manures; fresh material can burn plant roots.

Agricultural by-products. These vary from region to region; lasting quality depends on the material. Most are sold in bulk rather than packaged. Examples are ground corncobs, mushroom compost, apple or grape pomace, hulls from various nut crops, and cotton gin trash.

Pine needles. Appearance is pleasant, permeability is excellent, and the needles will last for several years. Acid reaction may be a bonus in all but acid-soil regions.

Grass clippings. To be successful, these need careful management to prevent compaction into a smelly, water-repellent mat. Spread a thin (½- to 1-inch-deep) layer of clippings; let this layer dry before you add another thin layer.

Leaves from trees. Their main advantage is availability; their chief drawback is that they can be blown around by the wind. If you use leaves, choose those with thicker textures (such as the leaves of many oaks); they'll remain loose. Thin-textured leaves (maple, for example) can mat together when spread in layers and moistened.

Fertilizing

Nutrient needs vary from one ground cover to another. But the virtue of many of these plants is that they will perform well with little or no supplemental nutrition.

A workable rule-of-thumb is to assume that the woody, shrubby ground covers (especially those that are drought tolerant) have a fairly low nutrient need and may get along without any fertilizer at all. Perennial ground covers, on the other hand, often have a higher nutrient demand and may need at least an annual fertilizer application.

Soil type affects the need to fertilize. Heavier, claylike soils contain more nutrients (and hold dissolved nutrients from fertilizers longer) than do lighter, sandier soils. Ground covers in lighter soils, therefore, are more likely to need some periodic fertilizer boost.

What Fertilizer to Use

Plants need three major nutrients—nitrogen, phosphorus, and potassium. Most commercial fertilizers contain all three and are popularly known as "complete." Nutrient percentages are listed on the label—for example, 5-10-10, with nitrogen listed first, then phosphorus, and finally potassium.

Nitrogen is water soluble and is depleted by plant uptake, watering, and precipitation. Phosphorus and potassium do not leach through the soil; to be effective beyond the top few inches, they must be dug into the root zone—ideally before you plant.

For ground covers, you can use dry granules or liquid preparations.

Dry granular fertilizers. Most granular fertilizers are scattered onto the soil, lightly scratched in, and then watered. The effect may last from several weeks to several months, depending on the type of nitrogen the fertilizer contains.

Fertilizers containing nitrogen in nitrate form are the fastest acting (and shortest lasting); if nitrogen is in ammonium or organic form (or derived from urea), the fertilizer will be slower to act but more sustained.

Controlled-release fertilizers contain dry, soluble nutrients in small pellets covered with a permeable membrane; a small amount of nutrients is leached from each pellet every time you water or rain falls. Depending on the product, these fertilizers last from 3 to 8 months after being lightly scratched into the soil.

Liquid fertilizers. These provide nutrients immediately but, because they're already in solution, they leach through soil fairly soon after application. Some of these fertilizers are concentrated solutions that you dilute in water; others are dry concentrates that you dissolve in water. A fertilizer injector (see page 25) makes it easy to apply liquids over a large planting, especially if used in conjunction with a drip-irrigation system.

When to Fertilize

Your first opportunity to apply fertilizer is when you prepare soil for planting (see page 21). This is the best time to add phosphorus and potassium—the two major nutrients that do not leach into the soil from surface application. By digging such fertilizers into the soil, you put these nutrients where roots can contact them.

You can use a "complete" fertilizer, or you can add formulas that contain only phosphorus and potassium. Whatever your choice, follow package directions for the amount to apply.

For established ground cover plantings, the best time to apply supplemen-

tal nutrients is just before the growing season. Fertilizer applied then (or just as growth begins) will provide nutrients for the year's major growth push.

If your planting seems to be standing still, with little or no new growth and perhaps a pale or spindly appearance, lack of nutrients (usually nitrogen) may be the cause. An application of liquid fertilizer will give the quickest results.

Good Grooming Practices

Even though a ground cover requires less routine maintenance than a comparable patch of lawn, there's still a need for periodic grooming to keep the planting looking its best.

Listed below are the most commonplace grooming routines. Note that each one doesn't apply to all ground covers; therefore, your total maintenance list will be shorter. Most of these routines are seasonal in nature. What you do—and when and how often you do it—depend on the ground cover you're growing.

Weeding. This is an "as-needed" chore, one whose frequency can be greatly reduced by the use of some good gardening practices.

Before planting, thoroughly weed the area (for more information, see page 21). After planting, one of the most effective ways to control weeds is a mulch (see page 27) spread to a depth of an inch or more over the soil between plants. This layer prevents most weed seeds from germinating—essentially making them too deeply "planted" to sprout and grow.

If you're concerned that you'll get an ample weed crop regardless, apply a preemergence herbicide to the bare earth just after planting. It will inhibit the germination of weed seeds and stop the growth of the embryonic plants.

Some preemergence herbicides are granules you apply to the soil and disperse with water; others are liquid concentrates diluted in water and sprayed on the soil. Check labels for a list of weeds controlled as well as for directions and cautions.

After applying a preemergence herbicide, you can follow up with a mulch. If weeds persist, hand-pulling is the most effective control if the crop is light.

For a serious weed infestation, you may be able to use a selective herbicide as long as you're certain it won't harm your ground cover. Carefully read product labels to learn which ornamental plants are unaffected by a particular selective herbicide, as well as to determine which weeds will be killed.

Edging. A number of ground covers will attempt to expand their territories unless you restrict them from time to time. Shrubby ground covers with stems that grow horizontally will need to be headed back into bounds whenever they stray. The sooner you do this, the less apparent the pruning.

For ground covers that spread by underground stems or that stake out new territory by rooting along stems that touch soil, you may be able to control spread by trimming the edges with pruning or hedge shears.

But if growth goes significantly beyond bounds, a spade or shovel may be your best pruning tool. Slice back to the desired edge; then dig out portions that have grown too far.

Pruning to shape. Some shrubby ground covers, normally low growing, occasionally send out upright stems that spoil the evenness of the planting. As they develop, cut these stems back to the point of origin or to a horizontally growing lateral within the foliage mass.

Mowing. Some of the ground covers that root as they spread, or spread by underground stems into dense patches, become so thick and matted in time that only mowing will restore their attractiveness. Plants like ivy (*Hedera*) build up accumulated thatch beneath the foliage, noticeably raising the surface of the cover. Others, such as *Euonymus* and *Hypericum,* may become rangy and untidy.

Mow these ground covers with a heavy-duty power mower, set at 3 to 4 inches, just before the beginning of the growing season.

Rejuvenation. Various perennial ground covers may become crowded in time, causing a decline in performance (and attractiveness) as more and more plants in a given space compete for water and nutrients.

When this occurs, dig up the planting, amend the soil, and replant with the strongest divisions or with new plants. Do this at the best time of year for planting in your region (see page 22).

Pest & Disease Control

One criterion of a good ground cover is that it be relatively untroubled by pests or disease—or that any infestation will do little harm to health or appearance. Still, there may be times when a problem appears to be serious enough to call for some attempt at control.

First, realize that most pests have natural enemies that keep them in check most of the time. If you need to reduce an unusually heavy infestation, start with nonchemical controls that do the least harm to natural predators. Move on to a chemical preparation only if these first methods are ineffective.

If you resort to a chemical control, choose one that's known to treat your plant's particular problem. Follow the product's label directions exactly for application, disposal of any excess solution, and storage.

The chart below describes some of the most widespread pest and disease problems and lists some appropriate controls.

Dealing with Pests & Disease

Aphids	Up to ¼ inch in length, these soft-bodied insects may be green, pink, red, brown, or black. Some have wings, others are wingless. They appear, often in large numbers, on new growth, which they pierce to suck the plant's juices. **Nontoxic controls:** Water-wash or spray with an insecticidal soap solution. **Chemical controls:** Malathion, pyrethrins (contact); Orthene (systemic).
Caterpillars	These wormlike pests, the larvae of different moths, chew holes in leaves, often reducing them to skeletons. They may be difficult to spot because they may assume the color of the host plant's foliage. **Nontoxic controls:** Hand-pick small infestations; or spray with a *Bacillus thuringiensis* preparation. **Chemical controls:** Diazinon, Sevin (contact); Orthene (systemic).
Mites	Near-microscopic spider relatives, mites proliferate in hot weather, gathering on leaf undersides where they suck plant juices. Look for yellow-stippled, dry-looking leaves. Defoliation can result if the infestation is unchecked. **Nontoxic controls:** Water-wash leaf undersides or spray with an insecticidal soap solution. **Chemical controls:** Kelthane (if available), Plictran, Vendex.
Powdery Mildew	This widespread disease (actually many different mildew species) appears as a gray to white, furry to powdery coating on buds, leaves, and stems. Some mildews attack new growth, others mature leaves. Most thrive in humid air but need dry leaves to become established. Some plants are more susceptible than others. **Nontoxic control:** Water-wash. **Chemical controls:** Folpet (contact); benomyl, triforine (systemic).
Scale	Adult scale insects live beneath rounded, waxy shells which adhere to leaves and stems; underneath their coverings, the insects suck plant juices. Eggs hatch beneath the shells; in spring or summer, young insects crawl to other parts of the plant and form their own shells. **Nontoxic controls:** Hand-pick or scrape, or apply an oil spray. **Chemical controls:** Diazinon, Malathion, Sevin (contact); Orthene (systemic).
Slugs & Snails 	These related mollusks (a slug is essentially a shell-less snail) feed on a wide variety of plants, consuming leaves by means of rasping mouths on their bodies' undersides. They thrive in moist weather and are especially active during cool, damp nighttime hours and on moist, sunless days. **Nontoxic controls:** Hand-pick or use saucers of beer set with rim at soil level. **Chemical controls:** Slug and snail baits.

Ground Covers A to Z

Enter the realm of ground covers and you'll discover a diverse and valuable assortment of garden problem solvers. On the following pages you'll find descriptions of the popular kinds that have proven their worth over many years in countless gardens. A few may be available primarily through specialty growers, but the majority are easy to obtain in the regions where they thrive.

Plants are listed in alphabetical order by their botanical names; beneath is the plant's common name, if it has one. In the first part of the detailed description that accompanies each entry, you'll find a complete plant profile—what the plant looks like, how tall and wide it grows, and how densely it covers. Popular hybrids and named varieties that differ in significant ways are also presented. Following that information are the plant's cultural and maintenance requirements.

For convenience in making a preliminary selection, consult the "thumbnail sketch" of each plant's cultural requirements, presented just below the name. This information can help you determine from the outset whether or not the ground cover is suitable for your particular situation.

■ *Zones* refers to the zones on the climate map on page 32 and specifies in which geographic regions the plant will grow.

■ *Type* tells you if the plant retains its leaves year-round (evergreen) or loses them over winter (deciduous). In addition, it specifies whether a plant has a permanent, woody structure (shrubs and most vines) or is a soft-stemmed perennial.

■ *Exposure* indicates whether the plant should receive sun, shade, or something in between. Degree of sun or shade tolerance can vary according to the climate; thus, the text may offer qualifications, for example, suggesting planting in partial shade where summer is hot. *Partial* shade—where the plant receives shade during part of a day (generally noon and afternoon)—has been differentiated from *light* shade, which indicates a bit of shade throughout the day.

■ *Water* needs vary, depending on the planting, your local climate, and your soil. Plants that must have a moist root zone need *regular* watering. If a plant will accept a bit of dryness between waterings, the need is *moderate.* Plants that require *little* water are the drought-tolerant individuals that will go for extended time periods between waterings.

■ *Spacing* refers to the recommended distances between plants, based on a plant's ultimate spread and its growth rate. The intervals should provide for complete cover in about 2 years.

Attractive entry landscape relies on just two ground covers: juniper (Juniperus) in foreground and, behind, a yellow-flowered carpet of spring cinquefoil (Potentilla tabernaemontanii).

Plant Hardiness Zone Map

The map shown below, devised by the U.S. Department of Agriculture, will help you determine the plants that will grow in your area. The zones are based on average expected low temperatures in winter; each zone encompasses a range of 10°F.

To use the map, locate the zone in which you live. Then consult the plant listings beginning on the facing page, noting the zone number or range given for the particular plant you're considering. That zone listing indicates the range of hardiness zones for which each plant is adapted. If your zone falls within the given range, the plant should grow in your region.

The map does have some obvious limitations. Any given hardiness zone will extend over a large geographical area.

For example, consider Zone 8, which includes the warm-humid North Carolina coast, the cool-humid Puget Sound, and the hot-dry Big Bend territory in Texas.

Moreover, a map such as this—based only on minimum expected temperatures—cannot possibly account for other significant aspects of climate that affect plant growth, such as humidity, expected high temperatures, and wind. Nor does it address variations in soils or the local microclimates that result from altitude, slopes, and morning and evening shadows from mountains.

Fortunately for the gardener, many plants will accept a variety of climates and still perform well. Where significant limitations do exist, such as in desert areas, we have noted them in the descriptions.

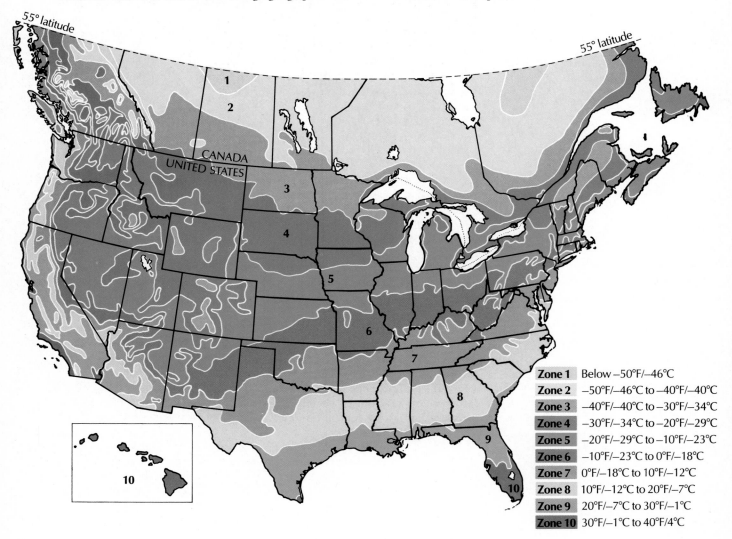

Zone 1	Below −50°F/−46°C
Zone 2	−50°F/−46°C to −40°F/−40°C
Zone 3	−40°F/−40°C to −30°F/−34°C
Zone 4	−30°F/−34°C to −20°F/−29°C
Zone 5	−20°F/−29°C to −10°F/−23°C
Zone 6	−10°F/−23°C to 0°F/−18°C
Zone 7	0°F/−18°C to 10°F/−12°C
Zone 8	10°F/−12°C to 20°F/−7°C
Zone 9	20°F/−7°C to 30°F/−1°C
Zone 10	30°F/−1°C to 40°F/4°C

ACHILLEA

YARROW

Zones: 4–10
Type: Evergreen perennials
Exposure: Sun
Water: Moderate
Spacing: 12 inches

The yarrows are easy, undemanding perennials, thriving in full sun and well-drained soil. In dry-summer regions, they appreciate moderate watering but can get by with less in cooler areas; established plantings will endure drought. Divide when plantings become overcrowded, showing diminished vigor or bare patches.

Foliage is finely cut to fernlike—gray or green and aromatic—forming low mats no higher than 4 to 6 inches. Tiny individual flowers are massed in flattened heads on stems rising above the foliage mass. Bloom starts in summer, lasting into fall. Shear off faded flowers to prolong bloom and keep appearance neat.

Greek yarrow (*A. ageratifolia*) forms a spreading mat of silvery leaves that may be lobed or nearly smooth edged. Stems 4 to 10 inches tall bear 1-inch clusters of white flowers. Silvery yarrow (*A. clavennae,* often sold as *A. argentea*) has silver gray, lobed leaves and ivory flowers in ¾-inch clusters atop 5- to 10-inch stems.

Woolly yarrow (*A. tomentosa*) has the lowest foliage of the three—a flat, dense mat of finely cut, furry, olive green leaves. Small clusters of bright yellow blossoms come on 6- to 10-inch stems; 'Primrose Beauty' has pale yellow flowers, while those of 'King George' are cream.

AEGOPODIUM PODAGRARIA

BISHOP'S WEED, GOUT-WEED
Pictured above and on page 12

Zones: 4–8
Type: Deciduous perennial
Exposure: Sun to shade
Water: Moderate
Spacing: 12 inches

Light green, divided leaves (each leaflet to 3 inches long) form a dense, even foliage mass about 6 inches high. "Ground elder," another common name, indicates foliage resemblance to that of box elder (*Acer negundo*).

Most commonly planted is *A. p.* 'Variegatum', the leaves of which are irregularly margined in white. Slender stems rise up to 18 inches above foliage mass in summer, bearing small, flat-topped clusters of insignificant flowers.

Adaptability and vigor are bishop's weed's strong points. It grows rampantly in sun, a bit more slowly in partial to full shade. Although it will take regular watering and good soil, it also performs well under less than ideal conditions.

Plantings spread by underground runners and can become invasive if not curbed by a barrier of concrete, metal, or wood extending below ground level. Mowing two or three times during the growing season maintains a neat appearance.

AGAPANTHUS

LILY-OF-THE-NILE

Zones: 9–10
Type: Evergreen perennial
Exposure: Sun to light shade
Water: Regular watering
Spacing: 12 inches

Several small versions of normally 3-foot-plus lily-of-the-Nile make attractive ground cover plantings when massed together. All form fountainlike clumps of strap-shaped leaves, above which rise stems bearing trumpet-shaped summer flowers in heads that resemble bursts of fireworks.

Plants grow quickly, but clumps increase slowly enough that they need infrequent division to relieve overcrowding.

Smallest is 'Peter Pan', with foliage to 12 inches high and blue blossoms atop 12- to 18-inch stems. White-flowered 'Peter Pan Albus' and 'Henryi' are only slightly larger. 'Rancho White' (also known as 'Dwarf White' and 'Rancho') has foliage that can grow to 18 inches with flower stems to 2 feet.

Aegopodium podagraria 'Variegatum'

AJUGA REPTANS

CARPET BUGLE

Zones: 4–10
Type: Evergreen perennial
Exposure: Sun to shade
Water: Regular watering
Spacing: 6 to 12 inches (18 inches for large types)

One of the most widely planted ground covers, carpet bugle has good-looking foliage and flowers; it performs well in sun and shade. Dark green, lustrous leaves with a quilted appearance form a thick, low foliage mat; leaf size is larger in shaded plantings. Blue flowers in 6- to 9-inch spikes appear in spring and early summer.

Many named varieties are sold (some under more than one name), offering variations in foliage color and plant size. 'Purpurea' ('Atropurpurea') has bronze-tinted green leaves, while 'Bronze Ripple', 'Metallica Crispa', and 'Rubra' have purplish or bronze foliage. Leaves of 'Variegata' are edged and splashed with creamy yellow; 'Burgundy Lace' ('Burgundy Glow') features white and pink variegation on reddish purple leaves.

Varieties with "giant" or "jungle" in their names have larger leaves and taller

Arctostaphylos uva-ursi

flower spikes; they also form higher foliage masses. Green-leaved selections include 'Giant Green' and 'Jungle Green'. 'Giant Bronze' and 'Jungle Bronze' have bronze-tinted foliage.

Carpet bugle grows rapidly, given regular watering and an annual application of fertilizer. Plants need well-drained soil; root rot and fungus diseases can be a problem among thick plantings in heavy, waterlogged soils. You can mow plantings after flowering to remove stems and tidy up appearance. Divide and reset plantings when vigor declines and bare patches appear.

ARABIS CAUCASICA

WALL ROCKCRESS

Zones: 6–9
Type: Evergreen perennial
Exposure: Sun to light shade
Water: Moderate
Spacing: 8 inches

Gray green, tongue-shaped leaves with toothed edges form thick mats of foliage whorls to 6 inches high. In early spring, small white flowers nearly cover the plantings. Several named varieties offer variations on this theme. 'Variegata' has cream white margins on gray leaves. 'Floreplena' has double blossoms; those of 'Pink Charm' and 'Rosabella' are pink.

Wall rockcress is best used in small areas. It grows loosely enough to make a good cover for spring-flowering bulbs. In hot-summer regions, plant in light shade. Renew plantings from rooted pieces or cuttings when ragged, bare patches appear.

ARCTOSTAPHYLOS

MANZANITA
Pictured above

Zones: Vary (none in desert)
Type: Evergreen shrubs
Exposure: Sun to partial shade
Water: Moderate
Spacing: 3 to 4 feet

The manzanitas forego showiness in favor of year-round attractiveness. Leaves are thick and leathery, glossy and fresh looking; many of the species have smooth, red to purple bark on main stems.

Appearing in late winter to early spring are pleasing but unspectacular flowers—clusters of small (less than ½ inch), urn-shaped blossoms in white or pink. These may be followed by small, round fruits.

Nearly all manzanitas are native to western North America and rarely are successful in other regions. The popular exception, though, is *A. uva-ursi*—bearberry or kinnikinnick. It also hails from northern latitudes in Europe and Asia and will grow in Zones 3–10 (West) and 3–7 (East). Plants form a foot-high, dense mat that spreads widely at a moderate rate, rooting along its stems. Inch-long leaves are bright green, turning to red in winter. White or pink flowers are followed by bright red to pink fruits.

Nurseries offer various selected forms. 'Massachusetts' and 'Alaska' have smaller, rounded leaves. 'Point Reyes' has plentiful, dark green foliage and is the best choice in regions with hot, dry summers. 'Radiant' has lighter green foliage and usually bears a heavy crop of red fruits. Bearberry excels on hillsides and in coastal climates.

Best soil for bearberry (and other manzanitas, below) is acid to neutral, well-drained sand to loam. If you plant in heavier soil, be careful you don't over-water; waterlogged soil leads to root rot. While plants are becoming established, water often enough to keep soil moist. In subsequent years, plantings will need water about once or twice a month, depending on summer heat.

New plantings establish slowly. Be sure to mulch thoroughly, preferably with sawdust or another wood product (see page 27), to suppress weeds and to encourage rooting along stems.

Gardeners in western North America can plant several other low, carpet-forming manzanitas. Similar to bearberry (and possibly a hybrid of it) is *A. media* (Zones 7–10). It's fast growing to 2 feet high, with darker foliage and brighter red branches.

Little Sur manzanita—*A. edmundsii*, Zones 8–10—is available in several selected forms. 'Danville' has rounded, light green leaves on a red-stemmed plant 4 to 24 inches high; pink flowers come in early winter. Fast-growing 'Carmel Sur' has gray green leaves and pink flowers; plants grow well under ordinary garden conditions. Variety 'Little Sur' grows slowly and remains very low; its leaves always have some red tints. Pink flowers come in early spring.

A. 'Emerald Carpet' (Zones 8–10) is noted for its shiny, bright green leaves that are only ½ inch long but plentiful; pink flowers bloom in early spring. Growth is especially uniform, remaining about 12 inches high.

ARCTOTHECA CALENDULA

CAPE WEED

Zones: 9–10
Type: Evergreen perennial
Exposure: Sun
Water: Moderate to little
Spacing: 18 inches

So easy to grow and tough enough to be called indestructible, Cape weed excels in sunny locations where you need a low, fast-growing cover—even on hillsides and where soil is poor. Elongated, gray green leaves are deeply toothed, forming a thick cover under 12 inches high. Yellow, 2-inch, gazanialike flowers can appear throughout the year, with heaviest bloom in spring.

The rapidly spreading plants are not for confinement in small spaces; they can be invasive (but easy to remove) in some situations. After planting, give regular watering until plants become established. Thereafter, water needs are moderate to low. Plants may be damaged by frosts in Zone 9 but will recover rapidly.

ARDISIA JAPONICA

Zones: 8–9
Type: Evergreen shrub
Exposure: Shade
Water: Regular watering
Spacing: 18 inches

Elegant foliage and seasonal color recommend ardisia for small, shaded areas. Leathery, 4-inch, oval leaves are bright green and glossy, clustered toward branch tips on upright stems 6 to 18 inches high. In fall, tiny white flowers appear in small clusters among the leaves, then produce bright red, pea-size fruits that remain through winter untouched by birds.

Plants prefer acid to neutral soil, in which they will spread by underground stems at a slow to moderate rate.

ARENARIA BALEARICA

CORSICAN SANDWORT

Zones: 6–10
Type: Evergreen perennial
Exposure: Shade
Water: Regular watering
Spacing: 6 inches

Dense, ground-hugging growth of tiny leaves gives the appearance of a velvet carpet. Late spring and summer bring forth small, circular white flowers nestled on top of the foliage mat.

Stems root as they spread, sometimes becoming invasive under preferred conditions of shade and moisture. Best uses are as small-space lawn (it will endure light foot traffic) or as green filler between stepping-stones.

ARENARIA VERNA

(See Sagina Subulata)

ARMERIA MARITIMA

COMMON THRIFT, SEA PINK
Pictured below and on page 1

Zones: 3–10
Type: Evergreen perennial
Exposure: Sun
Water: Moderate
Spacing: 6 to 12 inches

Clumps of stiff, grasslike leaves form foliage mounds about 6 inches high and 12 inches across. Slender stems rise above the leaves, bearing tight, round clusters of pink or white flowers. Where frosts are rare or absent, plants can flower throughout the year. In other regions, bloom season is spring. The individual-clump effect resembles that of pink-flowered chives;

Armeria maritima

closely planted, foliage appears as a shaggy, flowering turf.

Root rot can be a problem if water lingers for any time at bases of plants. Well-drained soil is best, in which plants can take regular watering (even though they thrive with lesser amounts). In heavier soils, though, water moderately. After bloom season, shear off spent flowers.

ARTEMISIA CAUCASICA

SILVER SPREADER

Zones: 5–9
Type: Evergreen perennial
Exposure: Sun
Water: Moderate to little
Spacing: 12 to 24 inches

Silvery gray green, finely cut leaves glisten with a silken sheen on dense, spread-

Asarum caudatum

ing plants that grow no higher than 6 inches. Small yellow summer flowers are insignificant.

Silver spreader prefers well-drained soil; it tolerates heat, cold, and infrequent watering in summer. Established plantings are fire retardant.

ARUNDINARIA PYGMAEA

Zones: 7–10
Type: Evergreen perennial
Exposure: Sun to partial shade
Water: Regular watering
Spacing: 12 to 24 inches

Some nurseries still sell this bamboo as *Sasa pygmaea,* but under either name it is an aggressively spreading plant that grows no higher than 18 inches. Bright green leaves are narrow, to 5 inches long, borne on pencil-thick stems.

Due to its invasive nature, plants should be confined with sturdy underground barriers of concrete, metal, or wood. This invasiveness, though, makes it an excellent plant for controlling erosion on sloping land.

Plants from crowded containers will begin to colonize faster than will small, unestablished plants. If appearance becomes shabby or leggy in a few years, mow it to restore attractiveness.

ASARUM CAUDATUM

WILD GINGER
Pictured at left

Zones: 5–9 (West, except desert)
Type: Evergreen perennial
Exposure: Shade
Water: Regular watering
Spacing: 12 inches

When given the shade and moisture it prefers, wild ginger makes a handsome ground cover. Heart-shaped, dark green leaves are 2 to 7 inches across, each carried on a leaf stalk to 10 inches high; leaves overlap to form a lush, ground-concealing carpet. Unusual reddish brown, bell-shaped flowers appear in spring but are mostly hidden beneath the foliage.

Wild ginger needs ample moisture for good growth. Plants grow best in rich, moisture-retentive soil with regular watering, though they also will thrive in well-drained soils with plenty of water and periodic applications of fertilizer. Slugs and snails consider wild ginger a delicacy.

ASPARAGUS DENSIFLORUS 'SPRENGERI'

SPRENGER ASPARAGUS

Zones: 9–10
Type: Evergreen perennial
Exposure: Sun to light shade
Water: Regular watering
Spacing: 2 to 3 feet

Though it is most frequently seen as a container plant, Sprenger asparagus can serve well as a billowy, mounding ground cover. The many-branched stems, 3 to 6 feet long, fountain outward from a central root mass; each branch carries many bright green, needlelike "leaves" (which actually are modified branches) to 1 inch long, giving a distinctive feathery appearance. Small, pinkish white flowers form pea-sized berries that become bright red at maturity.

Sprenger asparagus thrives in full sun where summers are cool; in hot-summer regions, give it partial or light shade (too much shade, however, results in yellowed foliage).

Plants will withstand infrequent watering, but regular water produces the best appearance. In early spring, apply fertilizer and trim out old stems (or shear entire planting); new growth will quickly renew the planting.

ATRIPLEX SEMIBACCATA

AUSTRALIAN SALTBUSH

Zones: 8–10
Type: Evergreen shrub
Exposure: Sun
Water: Moderate to little
Spacing: 3 feet

Its ability to withstand heat, drought, and poor or alkaline soil—from desert to seashore—makes Australian saltbush a good ground cover candidate for hillside situations and garden fringe areas in dry-summer regions. Established plantings also are fire retardant. Gray green leaves to 1½ inches long densely clothe branches that rise to 12 inches high and spread to 6 feet or more. Flowers are insignificant.

BACCHARIS PILULARIS

COYOTE BRUSH, DWARF CHAPARRAL BROOM
Pictured at right

Zones: 8–10 (West)
Type: Evergreen shrub
Exposure: Sun to light shade
Water: Moderate to little
Spacing: 2 to 3 feet

Although native to coastal California, coyote brush thrives in a wide range of soils and climates—from sandy soil and coastal fog to heavy or alkaline soil and desert heat. Mounding shrub reaches 8 to 24 inches high and may spread to 6 feet or more.

Glossy, ½-inch toothed leaves densely clothe the branches. Because female plants produce cottony seed heads (which can be messy as the wind disperses them), look for named selections which are propagated from seedless male plants. 'Twin Peaks' ('Twin Peaks #2') grows at a moderate rate, bearing small, dark green leaves. 'Pigeon Point' has larger, lighter green foliage; it grows

Baccharis pilularis

faster than 'Twin Peaks' and spreads farther.

Coyote brush will accept regular watering but doesn't require it. In coastal and inland areas, established plants will thrive during the dry months with no water; in regions with extremely hot summers, occasional watering may be needed.

Prune annually, before growth starts, to improve appearance. Remove upright or arching stems that disrupt evenness of planting's surface, and thin out old, woody branches.

BERGENIA

Pictured on page 38

Zones: 3–10 (except desert)
Type: Evergreen perennials
Exposure: Partial or light shade
Water: Regular to moderate
Spacing: 18 inches

Handsome, bold glossy leaves make a striking contrast to finer-textured plants.

Individual leaves are broad, rounded, and rubbery textured; they are carried on short leaf stalks that grow from clumping rootstocks. Foliage mass rises to 18 to 24 inches.

Two species are widely available. Rounded leaves of *B. cordifolia* reach 10 inches in length, with wavy, toothed edges and heart-shaped bases; clusters of 1½-inch pink flowers appear in spring on stems that are partially obscured by the foliage. Winter-blooming *B. crassifolia* features pink, lilac, or purple flowers on stems that rise above the foliage; individual leaves are broadly oval, to 8 inches long with wavy margins.

Bergenia plantings look best when they are grown in good soil and receive regular watering. But plants will endure poor soil and infrequent watering; in cool-summer regions, they will get through summer with little supplemental water even when planted in full sun.

Remove dead leaves annually; divide and replant when clumps become crowded and rootstocks rise well above the ground. Slugs and snails can be troublesome.

Bergenia crassifolia

BOUGAINVILLEA

Zone: 10
Type: Evergreen shrubby vine
Exposure: Sun
Water: Regular to moderate
Spacing: 6 to 8 feet

Although bougainvillea is most often grown as a vine, displaying flashy colors on walls, pergolas, and roofs, its vining habit can be put to use as a ground cover. Bougainvillea is particularly effective covering sloping land. Because of its thorns, it makes a fine barrier.

Stems are woody and sprawling, armed with needlelike spines; dark green leaves are oval to nearly heart shaped, 2 to 3 inches long. Showy spring and summer "flowers" actually are colorful, papery bracts surrounding the tiny, incon-spicuous real flowers. Familiar varieties feature bracts of red, violet, or purple, but new hybrids are available in yellow, bronze, pink, orange, lavender, white, and multicolor combinations. Some are shrubby rather than vining; for best ground cover, select a vining plant.

Planting requires particular care. Bougainvillea roots are sensitive to disturbance or exposure, and roots don't compact container soil into a firm mass.

If you're planting from a plastic container, cut out its bottom and place the container in the planting hole; then carefully slit one side and remove the plastic, filling in around the root ball with soil. If the container is metal, punch numerous holes in its sides and bottom, then plant the entire can; in time, the metal will rust.

Plants grow rampantly with regular watering but will thrive with moderate amounts. In midsummer, cut back on water to increase bloom production. Plants respond to applications of fertilizer in spring and again in summer. Try to train upward-growing shoots to a horizontal position; if that fails, cut them back to spreading stems.

CALLUNA VULGARIS

SCOTCH HEATHER
Pictured on pages 17 and 18

Zones: 5–9 (except desert)
Type: Evergreen shrub
Exposure: Sun to light shade
Water: Regular watering
Spacing: 12 to 18 inches

This species and its numerous varieties are true heathers; for a similar plant often incorrectly called heather, see *Erica* (heath) on page 45.

Fine textured is the term that describes Scotch heather. Tiny, scalelike, dark green leaves clothe branches of the mounded to spreading plants. Spikes of small, bell-shaped flowers appear at the tips of stems—usually in middle to late summer, although some varieties bloom in fall. Flowers come in pink, lavender, and purple shades, as well as white.

Among the many varieties available, plant habit varies from upright to mounding to spreading. Good choices among spreading kinds include 'Aurea', with purple flowers and gold foliage that turns red brown in winter; 'David Eason', red purple flowers in fall; 'J. H. Hamilton', double pink blossoms; 'Mrs. Ronald Gray', to 3 inches high with red purple flowers; and 'Nana', to 4 inches high with purple blooms.

Scotch heather needs acid, well-drained, moist soil. It performs best in regions that have cool, moist summer weather. You may be able to grow plants successfully in dry-summer areas if you water frequently so that soil never dries. With such regular watering, apply acid fertilizer in late winter and again in late spring. In hot-summer areas, the similar *Erica* is easier to grow.

CAMPANULA

BELLFLOWER
Pictured at right and on page 6

Zones: 4–10 (West), 4–9 (East)
Type: Evergreen perennials
Exposure: Sun to light shade
Water: Varies
Spacing: 12 inches

Of the many *Campanula* species, two are spreading plants that make excellent ground covers in small areas.

Dalmatian bellflower, *C. portenschlagiana* (often sold as *C. muralis*), forms a dark green foliage mass 4 to 7 inches high. Its long-stalked leaves are nearly round, with wavy, deeply toothed edges. From mid-spring through summer, foliage is nearly obscured by the inch-long, bell-shaped flowers of bright violet blue. The mounding plants spread at a moderately rapid rate.

Serbian bellflower, *C. poscharskyana,* spreads more rapidly with long, trailing, many-branched stems. Somewhat lighter green, its heart-shaped leaves vary from about 1 to 3½ inches long. From spring to early summer, star-shaped, blue to lavender blossoms dapple the plants; blooms up to an inch in diameter grow on stems that may reach 12 inches in height.

Both bellflowers perform best in good, well-drained soil with regular watering, although Serbian bellflower will endure infrequent watering (but at the expense of good appearance). They grow everywhere in partial or light shade but will take sunny locations wherever summer is cool or mild. Slugs and snails may be a problem.

CARISSA MACROCARPA

NATAL PLUM

Zones: 9 (warmest areas)–10
Type: Evergreen shrub
Exposure: Sun to shade
Water: Moderate
Spacing: 3 feet

In frost-free (or nearly frostless) regions, the low, spreading forms of Natal plum are among the most handsome and adaptable plants available for ground cover planting. Rich green, glossy, oval leaves to 3 inches long clothe stems that are armed with slender, sharp spines.

Highly fragrant, star-shaped, 2-inch flowers appear throughout the year, followed by 1- to 2-inch, plum-shaped green fruits that turn red when ripe; fruits (with cranberrylike flavor) are edible fresh or preserved. Because of its spines, Natal plum makes a good barrier planting.

Nurseries may offer several spreading varieties. 'Green Carpet' has small leaves on a plant that may reach 1½ feet high. 'Horizontalis' may reach 2 feet high, with more vinelike growth. 'Prostrata', despite its name, may reach 2 feet high, with occasional upright stems that should be cut

out to keep planting low. 'Tuttle' (sometimes sold as 'Nana Compacta Tuttlei') is a mounding-spreading shrub to 3 feet high and 5 feet wide that produces a heavy crop of flowers and fruit.

Natal plum thrives in direct coastal conditions and is fairly drought tolerant in a coastal climate. Away from the coast, it will need moderate watering during dry months. Plants tolerate soils from sandy to claylike.

CEANOTHUS

WILD LILAC
Pictured on pages 9 and 40

Zones: 8–10 (West, except desert)
Type: Evergreen shrubs
Exposure: Sun to partial shade
Water: Moderate to little
Spacing: 3 to 5 feet

The wild lilacs of western North America (no relation to true lilacs) are cherished for their early spring contribution of blue shades to the landscape. Most are medium-size to large shrubs, but the naturally prostrate growth of two species has established them as ground covers.

Campanula poscharskyana

Point Reyes ceanothus, *C. gloriosus,* grows well in coastal and cool-summer areas but usually does not succeed where summer is hot. The basic species has inch-long, dark green, oval leaves with spiny margins; tiny, light blue blossoms are in rounded clusters 1 inch wide. The plant spreads widely but grows only 1 to 1½ feet high.

Variety 'Anchor Bay' is the same height but less spreading, with especially dense foliage cover and slightly deeper blue flowers. Deep violet blue blossoms distinguish *C. g. exaltatus* 'Emily Brown', which has hollylike, 1-inch leaves on a 2- to 3-foot-high plant.

Leaves that are glossy, 2-inch ovals give a different texture to Carmel creeper, *C. griseus horizontalis.* This fairly wide-spreading plant grows 1½ to 2½ feet tall, bearing 1-inch clusters of light blue flowers.

Pale blue-flowered 'Hurricane Point', an especially wide-spreading variety, grows to 3 feet high. 'Yankee Point' makes a high cover, 3 to 5 feet tall, clothed in slightly smaller, darker green leaves; its blossoms are medium blue.

In general, *Ceanothus* species are susceptible to root rot in poorly drained

Ceanothus

soils, especially in hot-summer regions. These ground cover types are more tolerant of normal garden conditions than most, particularly in coastal and cool-climate gardens, but the safest approach is to give them well-drained soil and moderate watering (after plants are established).

A notable exception to the general rule is 'Emily Brown', which will grow in heavy soil in coastal regions with regular watering.

CERASTIUM TOMENTOSUM

SNOW-IN-SUMMER

Zones: 3–10
Type: Evergreen perennial
Exposure: Sun
Water: Moderate
Spacing: 12 to 18 inches

Small, snowy white flowers nearly obscure this plant's foliage from late spring into summer, providing its descriptive common name. During the rest of the year, it's an attractive foliage mat 6 to 8 inches high, with tufts of narrow, silver gray leaves less than an inch long. Rapid growth may achieve a 2- to 3-foot spread from one plant in a year.

Snow-in-summer thrives in many climates, from cool coastal to simmering desert. Plants need well-drained soil to offset root rot; in hottest summer regions, plant in light shade. Plants grow most rapidly with regular watering but will tolerate considerable drought. Shear off flower stems or mow entire planting after blossoms have faded.

Snow-in-summer is not long-lived as a ground cover; plantings may begin to get patchy after several seasons. When that occurs, it's best to start over with divisions or cuttings.

CERATOSTIGMA PLUMBAGINOIDES

DWARF PLUMBAGO
Pictured on facing page

Zones: 6–10 (except desert)
Type: Deciduous perennial
Exposure: Sun to partial shade
Water: Moderate
Spacing: 18 inches

Dwarf plumbago provides a spot of vivid blue from midsummer to mid-autumn,

when cool tones are most welcome in the garden. Loose clusters of intense blue, ½-inch flowers appear at the ends of 6- to 12-inch, wiry stems; leaves are 3-inch ovals of bronze-tinted green that turn bronzy red with frost.

Best flower production is in regions having a long growing season. Plants spread fairly rapidly by underground stems to form a dense, soil-knitting cover.

Plants will grow in a wide range of soils from claylike to sandy, spreading more rapidly in lighter soils. After the flowering period, annual growth becomes shabby looking; shear or mow the planting before new growth begins. In time, overcrowding may cause plantings to decline in vigor or start to die out in patches. When this occurs, dig and replant with rooted stems.

CHAMAEMELUM NOBILE

CHAMOMILE

Zones: 3–10
Type: Evergreen perennial
Exposure: Sun to light shade
Water: Moderate
Spacing: 12 inches

Low, dense growth and finely cut, bright green leaves make chamomile useful as a lawn substitute and for growing between paving stones. Stems root as they spread along the ground, forming a solid cover. Aromatic foliage emits a pleasant scent underfoot.

Plantings may grow up to 12 inches high; in summer, they bear either small, buttonlike yellow flowers or, in some forms, small white daisy blossoms. Dried flowers were the source of traditional (rather bitter) chamomile tea. 'Treneague' is a nonflowering variety. Some nurseries still sell these plants under the old name *Anthemis nobilis.*

Plants grow well in light to heavy soil. An occasional mowing (particularly after the flowering period) keeps plantings neat. The flowerless 'Treneague' stays low and even without mowing.

CISSUS

Zones: 9–10
Type: Evergreen woody vines
Exposure: Sun to shade
Water: Moderate
Spacing: 5 feet

Several *Cissus* species—warm-climate relatives of familiar Boston ivy and Virginia creeper (*Parthenocissus* species)—make handsome ground and bank covers in regions where frost is light or nonexistent.

Kangaroo treebine, *C. antarctica,* has glossy, spear-shaped leaves to 3½ inches long with toothed edges and prominent veins; vigorous plants, with stems to about 10 feet long, make an elegant foliage cover.

Rampant *C. hypoglauca* may achieve a 15-foot spread in one season (established plants may reach 30 feet or more). Its highly polished, bronze-tinted leaves are divided into five rounded, leathery leaflets, each to 3 inches long; new growth is covered with rust-colored fuzz.

Delicate-appearing *C. striata* has foliage like Virginia creeper: leaves divided into three to five leaflets, each 1 to 3 inches long. The dark green, leathery foliage contrasts pleasantly with reddish stems on a plant that may reach 20 feet in spread.

None of the *Cissus* species is particular about soil. Growth generally is vigorous without supplemental fertilizer.

CISTUS SALVIIFOLIUS

SAGELEAF ROCKROSE

Zones: 8 (warmest parts)–10 (West)
Type: Evergreen shrub
Exposure: Sun to light shade
Water: Moderate to little
Spacing: 3 feet

A native of Mediterranean lands, sageleaf rockrose adapts well to dry-summer climates from seacoast to desert. Dense, shrubby growth reaches to 2 feet high, spreading to about 6 feet and rooting occasionally where stems contact soil.

Ceratostigma plumbaginoides

Wrinkled, wavy-edged leaves are light grayish green to an inch long. In spring, plants are covered with 1½-inch, yellow-centered white flowers. Each bloom lasts only a single day, but many buds keep a good display going for a month or more.

Sageleaf rockrose grows in a variety of soils—good or poor, claylike or sandy. It's a good choice for planting on sunny banks where its roots help control erosion. Although drought tolerant (needing just occasional summer watering in hot summer regions), it will take regular watering if soil drains well.

CONVALLARIA MAJALIS

LILY-OF-THE-VALLEY

Zones: 3–coldest parts of 9 (except desert)
Type: Deciduous perennial
Exposure: Shade
Water: Regular watering
Spacing: 6 inches (individual pips)

Lily-of-the-valley is renowned for its fragrant flowers—charming, pendant white bells in early spring on 6- to 8-inch stems. But the 8-inch, lance-shaped leaves are handsome in their own right. Plants will slowly spread into a thick cover that's an asset in a lightly shaded garden, in the deeper shade of north-facing walls, beneath deciduous trees (where they can endure root competition), or under choice evergreens, such as rhododendrons and pieris.

You can plant lily-of-the-valley from individual rootstocks (called pips), spacing them about 6 inches apart, or you can plant small clumps about 12 inches apart. Choose good soil and liberally amend it with organic matter. Give plantings an annual topdressing of leaf mold, compost, or other organic material after foliage dies down in fall and before spring growth begins.

CONVOLVULUS MAURITANICUS

GROUND MORNING GLORY

Zones: 8–10 (West, except desert)
Type: Evergreen perennial
Exposure: Sun
Water: Moderate
Spacing: 3 feet

Typical lavender blue, morning glorylike flowers adorn this 1- to 2-foot-high, spreading plant from late spring into mid-

Coprosma kirkii

fall. But unlike true morning glories (*Ipomoea*), these 2-inch flowers remain open during the day. Lax stems may extend to 3 feet or more, bearing softly hairy, rounded, gray green leaves to 1½ inches long.

Ground morning glory prefers light, sandy, or gravelly well-drained soil, although it can succeed in heavy soil if plants are not overwatered. Older plants may become woody and sparse; to prevent this, trim back older stems annually in late winter.

COPROSMA

Pictured above

Zones: 9–10 (West, except desert)
Type: Evergreen shrubs
Exposure: Sun to partial shade
Water: Moderate to little
Spacing: 2 feet

Two *Coprosma* species make fairly high, spreading ground covers bearing plentiful small, attractive leaves. Flowers are insignificant.

Inch-long, very narrow, yellow green leaves characterize *C. kirkii,* which

grows to 2 to 3 feet; its long branches angle upward from the base in a broad V-shape. Plants will control erosion on slopes and thrive in direct seacoast conditions. Slightly lower-growing *C. pumila* features broadly oval, shining, bright green leaves just under an inch long; 'Verde Vista' is a superior named variety.

Both species are drought tolerant when established and grow well in soils ranging from heavy to light. *C. pumila* will accept regular watering as well, although it doesn't need it.

CORNUS CANADENSIS

BUNCHBERRY

Zones: 3–6
Type: Deciduous perennial
Exposure: Shade
Water: Regular watering
Spacing: 12 inches

This ground-level dogwood is more exacting in its requirements than most other ground covers. But when conditions are suitable, it can cover great amounts of surface with an even carpet of broadly oval, 1- to 2-inch leaves in whorls atop 4- to 6-inch stems.

Spring flowers bloom at stem tips, the true flowers framed by four white, petal-like bracts that look like 1- to 1½-inch blossoms. Small, bright red, edible fruits appear in late summer to early fall. Foliage turns yellow in fall; then the entire plant dies back to ground level.

Basic requirements are moist, acid soil with plenty of organic matter. Given these conditions, bunchberry will spread by underground stems at a moderate rate. Sometimes, small pieces are hard to establish; for best success, transplant small clumps with a piece of rotten log with bark attached.

CORONILLA VARIA

CROWN VETCH

Zones: 3–10
Type: Deciduous perennial
Exposure: Sun to shade
Water: Moderate
Spacing: 12 inches

Use this clover relative on erosion-prone slopes and along the fringes of large gardens where its vigor and tenacity will outweigh its somewhat weedy appearance. It's not attractive for close-up planting, and its invasiveness will be a problem in well-organized gardens.

Spreading from underground roots, crown vetch sends up a thick cover of 2-foot, sprawling stems bearing compound leaves, each containing 11 to 25 oval, ½-inch leaflets. Clusters of small, pinkish lavender flowers form brown, fingerlike seed capsules. The entire plant dies down to roots for the winter.

Crown vetch performs best in full sun but will also grow satisfactorily in shade. It's not particular about soil type. For best appearance, mow planting in early spring; then fertilize and water to promote lush growth.

CORREA PULCHELLA

AUSTRALIAN FUCHSIA

Zones: 9–10 (West, except desert)
Type: Evergreen shrub
Exposure: Sun to partial shade
Water: Moderate
Spacing: 2 to 4 feet

Although not related to true fuchsias, these plants do have pendant, bell-shaped, 1-inch flowers that bloom at a distinctly unfuchsialike time of year: mid-fall to early spring. Three are suitable as ground covers, bearing rounded, inch-long leaves that have a dense, gray, feltlike covering on the undersides.

The most widely sold species is *C. pulchella*, which features light pink flowers. Plants grow to 2½ feet high and spread to 8 feet. 'Carmine Bells' has red blossoms on plants to 2 feet high; 'Ivory Bells' is similar except for flower color.

Good drainage is the key to success with Australian fuchsia. Sloping land and light soil (or poor, rocky soil) are entirely suitable. Plant in full sun where summer is mild; in hot-summer regions, plants may take full sun (although partial shade is safer), but they will not endure reflected heat from walls or pavement.

COTONEASTER

Pictured below and on pages 10, 18, and 44

Zones: Vary
Type: Evergreen and deciduous shrubs
Exposure: Sun to partial shade
Water: Moderate to little
Spacing: 3 to 5 feet

The rugged, undemanding cotoneasters provide special interest in two seasons. Springtime brings flattened clusters of small, wild roselike flowers in white or pale pink. In fall, bright red fruits (pea-size or larger) decorate the branches, usually remaining into winter.

All but one of the species described below have small (½- to 1-inch), oval leaves that range from bright to dark green on upper surfaces, gray to white beneath. In fall, the foliage of the deciduous species turns red.

Although cotoneasters will grow well in good soil with regular watering, they don't require such treatment. Poor soil and moderate watering are entirely suitable and, in fact, promote greater quantity of the decorative fruits.

All are best planted where they won't need frequent restrictive pruning; stubbed-off branch ends are unattractive. When pruning is necessary to limit spread, cut back to the branch juncture within the foliage mass so that the edge will retain an irregular, natural appearance. If vertical branches disrupt the desired horizontal plane, cut them back to their points of origin or to horizontal branches within the foliage.

Fireblight may cause a sudden wilting and blackening of cotoneaster stems and leaves; for remedies, see *Pyracantha*, page 69.

Two deciduous species offer distinctive growth habits. Creeping cotoneaster,

Cotoneaster microphyllus

C. adpressus (Zones 4–10), hugs the ground contours, growing slowly and remaining under 1 foot tall. Faster growing, to 18 inches high, with larger foliage and fruit, is *C. adpressus praecox* (sometimes sold as *C. praecox*).

Rock cotoneaster, *C. horizontalis* (Zones 4–10, except intermediate and low desert), has a very brief leafless period. Moderately fast growing, it may build to 3 feet high; the secondary branches along its main stems form a flat herringbone pattern. 'Variegatus' has white-edged leaves, while *C. h. perpusillus* is a lower-growing form with smaller leaves.

Among evergreen species, two spread widely but grow no higher than 6 inches. Bearberry cotoneaster, *C. dammeri* (sometimes sold as *C. humifusus*), Zones 5–10, grows rapidly, rooting as it spreads. The basic species has bright red fruits; selected varieties include 'Coral Beauty' (coral fruits), 'Royal Beauty' (deep red fruits), and 'Eichholz' (carmine red fruits and a scattering of colored leaves in fall). 'Skogsholmen' (Zones 6–10) has stiffer growth that can reach 1½ feet tall.

Narrow, willowlike leaves to 3½ inches long distinguish *C. salicifolius* 'Herbstfeuer' ('Autumn Fire') from the other ground cover types. Grown in Zones 6–10, it may lose part of its foliage over winter in the colder regions.

Similar to *C. dammeri* (and sometimes sold as a variety of it), *C.* 'Lowfast' (Zones 7–10) differs in several particulars: the ground cover reaches 1 foot high, its leaves are smaller, and growth is especially rapid. It's quite susceptible to fireblight in the warmest parts of the West Coast.

Taller still is rockspray cotoneaster, *C. microphyllus* (Zones 6–10). Main stems hug the ground, rooting as they spread, but secondary branches grow upright to 2 to 3 feet. Tiny, dark green leaves are slightly smaller than the rosy red fruits.

COTULA SQUALIDA

NEW ZEALAND BRASS BUTTONS

Zones: 6–10
Type: Evergreen to deciduous perennial
Exposure: Sun to light shade
Water: Regular watering
Spacing: 6 inches

Spreading plants with bronzy green, hairy, fernlike foliage hug the ground almost like turf. Against this fine-textured background come the summer flowers: petalless ¼-inch yellow daisies that look just like tiny brass buttons.

Reasonably rapid growth makes brass buttons suitable for large spaces as well as small; it also is attractive grown between paving stones. Plants may die to the ground over winter in Zones 6 and 7 but are evergreen in the warmer regions.

CYTISUS KEWENSIS

KEW BROOM

Zones: 6–8
Type: Deciduous shrub
Exposure: Sun
Water: Moderate
Spacing: 2 feet

Spreading, trailing green branches with tiny green leaves reach 4 feet or more in length but remain less than 12 inches high. In mid-spring, plants are decorated with a profusion of sweet pea-shaped, ½-inch blossoms in creamy white. If grown on a retained slope, branches will cascade, draping over the retaining wall.

Kew broom needs good drainage and will thrive in poor or sandy soils. Plants grow well in windy seashore gardens as well as inland locations.

Cotoneaster dammeri

DALEA GREGGII

TRAILING INDIGO BUSH

Zones: 9–10 (desert only)
Type: Evergreen shrub
Exposure: Sun
Water: Moderate to little
Spacing: 2 feet

This attractive desert native takes in stride the desert limitations of heat, dryness, and organically poor soils. Low, spreading branches are clothed with leaves consisting of small, pearly gray leaflets. Starting in spring and lasting until early summer, clusters of tiny lavender flowers decorate the gray surface. And good news for desert gardeners: the plant is not a favorite of rabbits.

Although established plants will tolerate drought, deep watering every other week encourages rapid growth.

DAMPIERA DIVERSIFOLIA

Zones: 9 (warmest parts)–10 (except desert)
Type: Evergreen perennial
Exposure: Sun
Water: Regular to moderate
Spacing: 12 to 18 inches

For small-scale use, even between paving stones, dampiera offers fine texture and arresting flower color. Ground-hugging plants consist of very narrow, inch-long leaves on trailing stems. In spring and summer, small, bright, deep blue blossoms that resemble those of the popular annual *Lobelia* appear.

Plants spread at a moderate rate both by underground stems and by rooting along stems that touch soil. Best growth is in well-drained sandy to loamy soil.

DUCHESNEA INDICA

INDIAN MOCK STRAWBERRY

Zones: 3–10
Type: Evergreen perennial
Exposure: Sun to shade
Water: Moderate
Spacing: 12 to 18 inches

At first glance, this ground cover would seem to be a strawberry: leaves are strawberrylike; plants spread by runners, rooting as they spread; and the ½-inch red fruits beg to be tasted.

But several details make the difference: the ½-inch flowers in spring and summer are yellow (not white), the fruits are nearly flavorless, and both flowers and fruits are carried above the foliage (whereas those of true strawberry nestle among or beneath the leaves). Foliage mass rises to about 6 inches in shade, lower in sun.

Growth is rapid and can be somewhat invasive, but it is easily controlled. Trim or mow annually in early spring to tidy up the appearance.

EPIMEDIUM

Zones: 3–9 (except desert)
Type: Evergreen perennial
Exposure: Shade
Water: Moderate
Spacing: 12 inches

A delicate tracery of handsome leaves and a pleasant display of spring flowers recommend the slow- to moderate-growing epimediums as small-scale ground covers. Use them in shaded or woodland gardens, along with rhododendrons, camellias, and other plants that prefer a somewhat acid soil.

From a dense network of underground stems rise wiry leaf stalks bearing leathery, 3-inch, heart-shaped leaflets—bronzy pink in new spring growth, turning bronze in fall. Flowers come in loose clusters, each blossom consisting of four sepals (in starlike arrangement) surrounding the small true flower, which usually has spurred petals.

Bishop's hat, *E. grandiflorum,* has flowers 1 to 2 inches across in a combination of red, lavender, and white; named varieties are available with flowers of white, pink, lavender, and red. Foliage and flowers reach about 12 inches high.

Yellow and red flowers distinguish *E. pinnatum,* which grows to 15 inches. Foot-tall *E. rubrum* has showy blossoms of crimson and yellow or white; named varieties with pink or white flowers are sold.

ERICA

HEATH
Pictured on page 17

Zones: Vary (none in desert)
Type: Evergreen shrubs
Exposure: Sun
Water: Regular watering
Spacing: 18 inches

Closely related to true Scotch heather (see *Calluna vulgaris,* page 38), the heaths share a close resemblance and similar cultural needs. Leaves are small and needlelike on dense, mounding-to-spreading plants. Flowers are small and bell to urn shaped in large clusters or spikes.

Colors include lilac, purple, pink shades, rosy red, bright red, and white. Season of bloom varies, depending on species or variety; by careful selection you may have heath in flower nearly year-round. Some gardeners create colorful patchwork plantings by mixing species and varieties that have different colors and bloom seasons.

Heaths need soil that is both moist and well aerated. The best soils are the well-drained sandy to loam types liberally amended with organic matter. Root systems are dense and matted; they'll control erosion on sloping land but are shallow and won't tolerate drought. Most heaths also require acid soil; the exception is *E. carnea* and its varieties, which will also grow well in soil that's neutral to slightly alkaline.

Heaths perform best in regions where the air is cool and moist, such as the maritime areas of the Northeast and

Northwest. Drier and hotter inland climates limit the potential for success; in such regions, plants should be lightly or partially shaded during summer. Shear off flowering stems after blooms fade. Plants seldom need fertilizer except, perhaps, in the poorest of sandy soils.

The most adaptable heath, *E. carnea* (sometimes sold as *E. herbacea*), grows in Zones 5–10 (West) and 5–8 (East). Flowering usually begins in early winter and, depending on variety, may last until early summer.

The basic species has rosy red flowers on a prostrate plant that sends upright branches to 16 inches. Lower-growing varieties include fast-growing 'Springwood' ('Springwood White') with white flowers and light green foliage; pure pink 'Springwood Pink'; and carmine red 'Vivelli', which undergoes a foliage color change to bronzy red during winter.

Dorset heath, *E. ciliaris,* grows in Zones 7–9 (West) and 7–8 (East). Rosy red flowers appear from midsummer into fall on a plant with light green leaves; blooming at the same time are the darker-foliaged varieties 'Mrs. C. H. Gill' (deep red) and 'Stoborough' (white). Except for 18-inch 'Stoborough', plants grow no higher than 12 inches.

Purple-flowered twisted heath, *E. cinerea,* and its scarlet-blossomed variety 'Atrosanguinea' bloom from early summer into fall on mounding, spreading plants that grow no higher than 12 inches. Those plants thrive in Zones 7–9 (West) and 7–8 (East). Also growing well in those zones is *E. tetralix* 'Darleyensis'; it has salmon pink blossoms from early summer into fall on an 8-inch, spreading plant with gray green foliage.

Erica 'Dawn' is an easy to grow hybrid for Zones 7–10 (West) and 7–8 (East). The plant grows in a spreading mound to 1 foot tall; its new growth is a contrasting golden yellow. Deep pink flowers begin in early summer and continue into fall.

Erigeron karvinskianus

ERIGERON KARVINSKIANUS

MEXICAN DAISY,
SANTA BARBARA DAISY
Pictured above

Zones: 9–10 (West), 9 (East)
Type: Evergreen perennial
Exposure: Sun
Water: Moderate to little
Spacing: 12 inches

Fine texture and a graceful appearance belie the toughness of this plant. Mexican daisy grows in light or heavy soil, accepts root competition from trees and shrubs, and tolerates drought when established (but it will accept routine garden watering). Stems may root when they contact soil; combined with rapid growth, this can make Mexican daisy an invasive (but easy to curb) ground cover.

Slender to wiry branching stems bear narrow, toothed leaves to an inch long. Pinkish white daisy flowers appear over a long period from late spring into fall. Spreading plants may reach 10 to 20 inches high; if they become lumpy or straggly, shear them back after flowering is over.

ERODIUM CHAMAEDRYOIDES

CRANE'S BILL

Zones: 8–10 (except desert)
Type: Evergreen perennial
Exposure: Sun to light shade
Water: Regular watering
Spacing: 6 to 12 inches

Here's an example of a rugged ground cover with a delicate appearance. Each plant produces a thick carpet of foliage to 6 inches high and about 12 inches across.

Long-stalked, roundish leaves are about ⅓ inch long with scalloped margins. Cup-shaped, ½-inch flowers bloom from mid-spring to mid-fall in white or rose pink; petals are veined in dark rose. The slender, pointed seed capsule that develops from each blossom's center gives the plant its common name.

Crane's bill prefers well-drained soil, but water often enough so the soil doesn't dry out. Fairly slow growth recommends the plant for use in small-scale areas.

EUONYMUS FORTUNEI

WINTER CREEPER
Pictured at right

Zones: 5–9
Type: Evergreen woody vine
Exposure: Sun to shade
Water: Moderate
Spacing: 2 feet

Winter creeper shares its growth habit with another popular ground cover, ivy (*Hedera,* see page 51). Juvenile growth is trailing and vinelike; it will cover the ground, rooting as it spreads. When it encounters vertical surfaces, it climbs upward, attaching with rootlets along stems.

In time, the vertical growth sends out shrubby branches, and plants grown from these will be shrubs rather than vines. Therefore, some named varieties of *E. fortunei* are vines, and some are shrubs. The following vining ground covers are all dense and neat, with polished foliage.

Common winter creeper, *E. f. radicans,* has thick, oval leaves to an inch long, forming a spreading, sometimes undulating, cover. Purple-leaf winter creeper, *E. f.* 'Colorata', makes a more even ground cover; its foliage turns purple during fall and winter.

'Gracilis'—often sold as *E. radicans argentea variegata, E. fortunei variegata,* or *E. f.* 'Silver Edge'—is a good small-space ground cover; its leaves are variegated with white or cream that turns pinkish in cold weather. Smallest of all is 'Kewensis' ('Minima') with pea-size, dark green leaves.

The various winter creepers tolerate a wide range of conditions: sun to shade, sandy to claylike soil, and regular to moderate watering. Plantings give solid cover after several years.

Euonymus fortunei 'Gracilis'

FESTUCA OVINA GLAUCA

BLUE FESCUE

Zones: 3–10 (West), 3–9 (East)
Type: Evergreen perennial grass
Exposure: Sun to light shade
Water: Regular to little
Spacing: 6 to 12 inches

Although the fescues are best known as turf grasses, blue fescue is strictly an ornamental plant used for pattern planting and ground cover. Plants form tightly knit tufts of soft but tough, needlelike leaves 4 to 10 inches long; an individual clump resembles a blue gray shaving brush. Flowering stems and seed heads are inconspicuous.

Use blue fescue on level ground or slopes in well-drained soil. Because clumps don't spread to form a solid cover, density depends on the spacing of clumps.

Desert plantings need regular watering; elsewhere, occasional watering is sufficient. If plantings become shabby in appearance, mow or shear the clumps to 2 inches high at any time. Eventually, the clumps will become overgrown and decline in vigor. When this occurs, dig them up, separate each clump into small divisions, and replant.

FRAGARIA CHILOENSIS

WILD STRAWBERRY

Zones: 6–10
Type: Evergreen perennial
Exposure: Sun to light shade
Water: Regular to moderate
Spacing: 12 to 18 inches

This true strawberry is native to the Pacific coast of North and South America, where it thrives in full sun in the maritime climate. It will also succeed in hotter, drier regions, but in these areas, it needs light or partial shade and regular watering. The glossy, dark green leaves have three toothed leaflets—similar to commercial strawberries, of which it's an ancestor.

Inch-wide white blossoms appear in spring, rarely followed by small red fruits that are edible but second-rate in flavor. In winter, the foliage becomes tinted with red. Plants grow 6 to 12 inches high, spreading rapidly by runners.

Mow foliage annually in early spring, before growth begins, to keep plantings renewed and prevent stem buildup. Later in spring, apply fertilizer to ensure vigorous, lush growth. If leaves become yellowish in late summer, apply iron sulfate to restore normal green color.

GALAX URCEOLATA

Pictured on page 50

Zones: 3–8 (except desert)
Type: Evergreen perennial
Exposure: Shade
Water: Regular watering
Spacing: 12 inches

For shady garden situations, it's difficult to find a more handsome ground cover. Slowly spreading clumps feature long-stalked, heart-shaped glossy leaves to 5 inches across; except in deeply shaded plantings, foliage turns bronze in winter.

Foliage height ranges from 6 to 9 inches; in summer, flower stems rise to

2½ feet, bearing small white flowers in foxtail fashion at their extremities.

Galax prefers acid soil liberally amended with organic matter. Plant it under dogwood, rhododendrons, azaleas, and pieris—shrubs and trees that appreciate the same conditions.

GALIUM ODORATUM

SWEET WOODRUFF
Pictured below

Zones: 5–10 (except desert)
Type: Evergreen perennial
Exposure: Shade
Water: Regular watering
Spacing: 12 inches

Plantings of fine-textured sweet woodruff always have a fresh appearance. Dense growth consists of narrow, bright green leaves that appear in closely set whorls of six to eight on slender stems 6 to 12 inches high. Tiny white, four-petalled flowers spangle this feathery cover in late spring and summer. The "sweet" of the common name comes from the dried foliage, which is used to flavor May wine.

When given good, slightly acid soil and regular watering, sweet woodruff will spread rapidly. Its noncompetitive root system makes it a good companion for shade-loving shrubs and trees. Healthy plantings can become somewhat invasive—both from spreading and from seedling plants.

GARDENIA JASMINOIDES 'RADICANS'

Zones: 8–10
Type: Evergreen shrub
Exposure: Sun to shade
Water: Regular watering
Spacing: 18 to 24 inches

Although blossoms lack the opulence of florists' gardenias, flowers on this plant exude the familiar fragrance. Spreading plants extend 2 to 3 feet, rising only 6 to 12 inches high; their small, oval leaves are glossy dark green, frequently streaked with white. Inch-wide white flowers appear throughout summer.

To succeed with this gardenia, you must pay close attention to its cultural needs. Give plants well-drained soil containing plenty of organic matter; set root balls a few inches above soil grade to avoid root rot.

Plants need heat for best performance. Choose a location in full sun in mild coastal regions and light shade (although perhaps with morning sun) in warm to hot inland areas. Apply acid fertilizer monthly during the growing season for best results. If leaves become chlorotic (yellow, with veins remaining green), apply iron chelate or iron sulfate.

GAULTHERIA

Zones: Vary
Type: Evergreen shrubs
Exposure: Light shade
Water: Regular watering
Spacing: 12 inches

Two woodland natives—one eastern, one western—make attractive, small-scale ground covers when used with other plants that share their need for moist, acid soil amended with plenty of organic matter. Both spread slowly by underground stems that produce upright branches bearing leathery, broadly oval, dark green leaves.

Taller of the two species, to about 8 inches, is western *G. ovatifolia* (Zones 6–9, except desert). Tiny white to palest pink, urn-shaped summer flowers mature in fall into pea-size, edible berries with a wintergreen flavor.

Eastern *G. procumbens* (Zones 4–9, except desert) is known as wintergreen, checkerberry, or teaberry, from the flavor of its similar scarlet fruits. Small summer blossoms are white, on a plant to about 6 inches tall.

Galium odoratum

Gazania

GAZANIA

Pictured above and on page 7

Zones: 9–10 (West)
Type: Evergreen perennial
Exposure: Sun
Water: Moderate
Spacing: Varies

Gazanias embody the essence of summer; their 3- to 4-inch daisy flowers bloom in warm tones of yellow, orange, red, copper, pink, cream, or white, often with a contrasting dark central eye. The major flowering period is late spring into midsummer, although in mildest areas gazanias will flower sporadically throughout the year. Blossoms open on sunny days, close when evening approaches, and remain closed during cloudy or overcast weather (except as noted below).

You can buy two types of gazanias—those that form compact clumps and those that spread by trailing runners. Clumping kinds are good for small-scale ground covers on level ground; space plants about 12 inches apart. Leaves typically are long and narrow, green on the upper surface and gray beneath.

Nurseries sell various named strains of mixed colors; the Chansonette, Daybreak (which open at dawn), and Mini-Star plants are more compact than other types. Several named hybrids are widely sold: 'Aztec Queen' (multicolored yellow and bronze flowers), 'Burgundy', 'Copper King', and 'Fiesta Red'. 'Moonglow' has double yellow flowers that open even on sunless days.

Trailing gazanias, planted 12 to 18 inches apart, will spread quickly to cover large areas, even on sloping ground. Foliage generally is silvery gray; flowers may be white, yellow, orange, or bronze. Among named varieties are orange 'Sunburst', yellow 'Sunglow', and green-leafed 'Sunrise Yellow'.

Gazanias are not particular about soil type. In desert regions they may need regular watering, but in areas with less intense heat, moderate watering is sufficient. Plantings (especially of clumping kinds) may decline in vigor or become patchy after 3 to 4 years. If this occurs, you can dig, divide, and replant in early spring.

Galax urceolata

GELSEMIUM SEMPERVIRENS

CAROLINA JESSAMINE

Zones: 8–10
Type: Evergreen woody vine
Exposure: Sun
Water: Regular watering
Spacing: 2 to 3 feet

In late winter and early spring, when floral displays are at a low ebb, Carolina jessamine covers itself with highly fragrant, 1- to 1½-inch, tubular yellow blossoms. During the rest of the year, an attractive appearance is maintained by the glossy, bright green, 1- to 4-inch oval leaves. Twining stems spread at a moderate rate. They'll try to climb any vertical supports they encounter—shrubs, trees, or fences.

As a ground cover, Carolina jessamine will mound up to 3 feet or more. Trim each year after flowering to help maintain the planting at an even height. Caution: All parts of the plant are poisonous.

GENISTA

BROOM
Pictured on page 8

Zones: 6–9 (except *G. lydia*)
Type: Deciduous shrubs
Exposure: Sun
Water: Little
Spacing: 2 feet

The various brooms offer an arresting display of small, sweet pealike yellow flowers in late spring. Tiny leaves may be oval or nearly needlelike and may not last through the growing season; however, the green stems give plants the appearance of being evergreen.

Smallest of the four ground cover species is *G. lydia* (sometimes sold as *Cytisus lydia*), which may reach 2 feet high with a spread to about 4 feet. It's also the least cold tolerant, growing in Zones 7–9 (except desert). Spanish broom, *G. hispanica,* grows 1 to 2 feet high and spreads widely; its spiny stems make it a good barrier plant.

Also wide spreading, to about 1½ feet high, is multibranched *G. pilosa,* which has gray green stems; selected for superior color and flower production is variety 'Vancouver Gold'. Winged branches of wide-spreading *G. sagittalis* give the foot-tall branches the appearance of being jointed. Its flowering period extends into summer.

The brooms are good choices for poor soil and for slopes or banks that receive little water. Plants thrive where summer is hot and dry (except for desert regions), as well as under coastal conditions.

GERANIUM

CRANESBILL

Zones: Vary
Type: Evergreen, deciduous perennials
Exposure: Sun
Water: Regular watering
Spacing: Varies

Although flowers are not as individually showy as those of the plants commonly called geranium (actually *Pelargonium*), the true geraniums offer a good show of color over a long period from spring to fall. Flowers are about an inch across, borne in clusters above a 6- to 10-inch cover of rounded leaves that are either lobed or finely cut.

Evergreen *G. incanum* grows in Zones 9–10 (except desert) but may be damaged by frost in colder parts of Zone 9. Finely cut foliage is the backdrop for magenta pink blossoms. Plants grow quickly, forming broad cushions; space them about 12 inches apart for cover.

Deciduous *G. macrorrhizum* (Zones 4–10) has aromatic, lobed leaves that take on tawny gold to russet shades in fall. Typical flower color is red, but with some searching you may find pink- or white-blooming varieties. Plants spread widely by underground stems; space them about 24 inches apart.

GREVILLEA

Zones: 9–10 (West, except desert)
Type: Evergreen shrubs
Exposure: Sun
Water: Moderate to little
Spacing: 3 to 4 feet

The two grevilleas suitable for ground cover are high, spreading shrubs. But large plantings escape appearing massive because of the fine texture created by the shrubs' needlelike leaves. Clustered flowers are narrow and tubular, with prominent stamens; hummingbirds find them enticing.

Woolly grevillea, *G. lanigera,* spreads to 10 feet, reaching 3 to 6 feet high. Gray green, ½-inch leaves are a good foil for the summer display of red and cream flowers.

Spring-blooming *G.* 'Noellii' features pink and white flowers against inch-long, bright green leaves. Plants may reach 4 feet high, spreading to 5 feet.

Although grevilleas will accept good, well-drained soil, they don't require it; they'll thrive in soils low in nutrients and organic matter.

Woolly grevillea excels in hot, sparingly watered situations; *G.* 'Noellii' needs moderate watering.

HEBE

Zones: Vary (West, except desert)
Type: Evergreen shrubs
Exposure: Sun to light shade
Water: Regular watering
Spacing: Varies

Wherever coastal weather dominates or influences a garden's climate, the hebes (sometimes still sold as *Veronica*) will flourish. And even in warmer, drier areas, they may succeed if planted in light shade. Plants need well-drained soil in all regions.

These ground covers bloom in summer; each blossom is tiny, with prominent, protruding stamens, but they appear grouped together in short spikes.

Taller of the two is *H. chathamica* (Zones 9–10), rising to 1½ feet and spreading to about 3 feet; space plants 18 inches apart. Lavender flowers appear against a backdrop of deep green, ½-inch oval leaves.

Creeping *H. pinguifolia* 'Pagei' (Zones 8–10) spreads to 5 feet but reaches only about 9 inches high; space plants 24 to 30 inches apart. Small, broadly oval, blue gray leaves are edged in pink; flowers are white, in plump spikes.

HEDERA

IVY
Pictured below and on pages 12 and 16

Zones: Vary
Type: Evergreen woody vines
Exposure: Sun to shade
Water: Regular to moderate
Spacing: 18 inches

If you need a rugged, adaptable ground cover that always appears neat and uniform and that will knit soil together with a multitude of roots (and control erosion on slopes), consider ivy.

When ivy is planted as a ground cover, the stems will root as they spread; if they contact vertical surfaces (for example, walls, fences, tree trunks, or shrubbery), they'll climb and cling with aerial rootlets. Ivy's leathery leaves are basically heart shaped with lobed margins; size and color vary.

Two species are widely available for ground cover planting. Algerian ivy, *H. canariensis,* is the larger of the two and grows in Zones 8–10. Its glossy leaves may reach 8 inches across; its variety 'Variegata' has green leaves edged with cream white.

Familiar English ivy, *H. helix,* grown in Zones 6–10, has dark green, nonglossy

Hedera canariensis

leaves to 4 inches across with conspicuous lighter veins. Nurseries may offer a few selected varieties; specialists will carry many more. 'Baltica' (a smaller-foliaged form whose leaves turn purple in winter) and 'Bulgarica' will grow in Zone 5.

'Hahn's Self-Branching' (sometimes sold as 'Hahn's Ivy' or 'Hahnii') has lighter green leaves and a more branching habit than the basic species. Other variations include those with small leaves, elongated foliage, and leaves with white, cream, or yellow variegation. Small-leafed types are effective as small-scale ground covers.

To get a planting off to a good start, prepare the soil as outlined on page 21. If you'll be planting on a slope, add organic amendment to each planting hole. When you plant, be sure that both the soil and the plants are thoroughly moistened.

Water regularly to get plants well established. Thereafter, Algerian ivy should receive regular watering. English ivy will have a better appearance in warm regions with routine watering, but plants are fairly tolerant of drought.

To keep plantings attractive and vigorous, apply a high-nitrogen fertilizer in early spring and again in midsummer. Hedge shears or a sharp spade will keep the edges of plantings neat.

After several years, a planting may build up a thick thatch of stems. When this occurs, you can shear back the ivy or mow it with a heavy-duty rotary mower; early spring is the best time, so new growth will quickly cover over.

Ivy is a notorious hiding and breeding place for slugs and snails, which may require control measures. In some areas, rodents take shelter in ivy plantings.

HELIANTHEMUM NUMMULARIUM

SUNROSE
Pictured on page 7

Zones: 5–10
Type: Evergreen shrublet
Exposure: Sun
Water: Moderate
Spacing: 24 to 30 inches

For small, sunny spaces (including sloping ground), sunroses offer fine-textured foliage spangled with a 2-month display of warmly colored flowers; bloom begins in middle to late spring, depending on the climate. Many varieties are sold; you can choose single or double flowers, and shades of pink, red, orange, copper, yellow, or white.

Each inch-wide blossom lasts only a day, but countless buds produce a good show throughout the bloom season. Narrow leaves, to an inch long, may be dark glossy green or nearly gray. Individual plants reach 6 to 8 inches high, spreading to about 3 feet.

Give sunroses well-drained soil and moderate watering in hot-summer regions, little water where summer is cool. Shear plants lightly after flowering to keep them dense and to encourage more blooms in late summer or fall. Where winter temperatures dip below freezing or where plants are exposed to wind and sun, cover plantings with evergreen boughs to prevent the leaves from drying out.

HELLEBORUS

HELLEBORE

Zones: Vary
Type: Evergreen perennial
Exposure: Shade
Water: Regular watering
Spacing: 12 to 18 inches

The elegant hellebores—including Christmas and Lenten roses—are clump-forming perennials that, when planted in mass, make handsome ground covers. Leaves are deeply lobed, each leaflet like the finger of an outstretched hand. Flowers resemble those of single roses, blooming in open clusters (except for *H. niger*) on stems that rise above the foliage.

Smallest of the species is *H. foetidus* (Zones 3–10), which has very dark green leaves divided into seven to eleven long, narrow leaflets; plants reach 1 to 1½ feet high. Light green, purple-margined, inch-wide flowers appear in late winter and early spring.

Christmas rose, *H. niger* (Zones 4–8, except desert), may bloom in December in warmer regions, or in late winter or early spring where winter is colder. Greenish white, 2- to 3-inch flowers, one to a stem, turn pinkish purple as they age. Each leaf contains seven to nine narrow, 9-inch leaflets; foliage may rise 1½ feet high.

Flowering in late winter to early spring, Lenten rose, *H. orientalis* (Zones 4–9), is available in white, pink, green, and purplish shades. The 2- to 3-inch blossoms are often spotted with dark purple; usually, they become greenish as they age. Foliage is the largest of all—five to eleven broad leaflets up to about 10 inches long.

Hellebores grow best in good soil with regular watering and an annual fertilizer application in early spring. But plants are unexpectedly rugged, persisting and performing satisfactorily with nothing more than moderate watering. Clumps never require dividing.

HEMEROCALLIS

DAYLILY

Zones: 3–10
Type: Evergreen to deciduous perennial
Exposure: Sun to light shade
Water: Regular to moderate
Spacing: 18 inches

Legions of gardeners grow daylilies for their lavish display of lilylike flowers in a wide range of colors and color combinations. But the foliage also is a landscape asset: narrow, curved leaves (an individual plant resembles a young corn plant) form fountainlike foliage clumps.

Massed together, daylilies create a handsome foliage cover (1 to 3 feet high, depending on the variety) with an arresting show of blossoms in late spring—and again in late summer to fall, if you choose kinds that rebloom.

As the name implies, each blossom lasts just a day, but the slender, branched flower scapes rising above the foliage carry many buds to provide blooms for a month or more. Specialists offer long lists of named varieties in yellow, orange, red, bronze, purple, pink, lavender, cream, or near white; some kinds have contrasting dark or greenish central bands, or eyes.

The size of plant, flower, and foliage can vary from miniatures with foot-high leaves to those with foliage rising to 3 feet and flower stems reaching 6 feet. For best appearance with a ground cover planting, choose a single variety or select varieties of similar size.

Some daylilies are completely deciduous; others are semi-evergreen or completely evergreen. Deciduous varieties are the best to plant in Zones 3–5; evergreen daylilies are best adapted to Zones 7–10. Semi-evergreen kinds prosper in Zones 5–9.

Daylilies appreciate good, well-drained soil but will thrive in a wide range of soil types. Plants compete well with some shallow-rooted trees. Regular watering helps plants maintain a good appearance throughout the season, but they'll endure with moderate amounts of water—even very little—in cool-summer areas. Apply fertilizer to plantings just as growth begins in spring; repeat in midsummer.

When clumps become overcrowded and decline in vigor and flower quality, dig and divide in early spring (colder regions) or fall (milder areas).

HERNIARIA GLABRA

GREEN CARPET, RUPTURE WORT

Zones: 5–10
Type: Evergreen perennial
Exposure: Sun to shade
Water: Regular watering
Spacing: 12 inches

Green carpet's tiny green leaves on creeping stems no higher than 3 inches create a mosslike effect. But unlike mosses, this plant will grow in full sun as

Hosta undulata

well as in shade. Use it in small spaces—creeping around rocks, between paving stones, or as a pattern plant with other low ground covers. The plant's greenish flowers are insignificant. In the colder zones, leaves turn bronzy red over winter.

HIPPOCREPIS COMOSA

Zones: 9–10
Type: Evergreen perennial
Exposure: Sun
Water: Regular to moderate
Spacing: 12 inches

The fine texture and soft appearance of this low ground cover mask a tough constitution. Growing to 3 inches high and

spreading widely, it can serve as a lawn substitute (even tolerating some foot traffic). Its roots will bind soil on sloping land, preventing erosion. And it will endure poor soil and little water.

Each leaf is composed of seven to fifteen tiny, bright green leaflets; the multibranched stems form a dense mat of foliage. Spring flowers are sweet pea-shaped, half-inch yellow blossoms in small clusters.

Despite its tolerance of adverse conditions, hippocrepis is better looking if planted in good soil and watered regularly. To keep a planting neat, mow it once a year after flowering is finished.

HOSTA

PLANTAIN LILY
Pictured below and on pages 13 and 53

Zones: 3–9 (except intermediate and low desert)
Type: Deciduous perennial
Exposure: Sun to shade
Water: Regular watering
Spacing: Varies

The many hostas (sometimes still sold under the old name *Funkia*) are premier foliage plants. Each makes a slowly expanding clump of long-stalked leaves that overlap in shingle fashion to become mounds of foliage. Slender stalks rise above the leaves (just barely above, in some varieties) in late spring or summer, bearing small, bell-shaped blossoms of white or lavender.

This is the basic theme, but the variations are seemingly endless. Leaves may be nearly round, heart shaped, or lance shaped, with smooth or quilted surfaces. Some plants have glossy foliage; others are dusted with a grayish bloom.

Foliage colors range from gray and blue to light and dark green. Variegated combinations abound, mixing white, cream, or yellow with the other colors. Even leaf size varies—from "giants" with leaves 9 inches or more in length to miniature varieties that make clumps no greater than 9 inches across.

The best way to choose a hosta is to visit a well-stocked nursery or consult a specialty catalog. You can then select for the foliage effect you desire; or pick several different kinds for a patterned planting.

All hostas prefer good soil and plenty of moisture. Plant in sun to moderate shade where summer is cool to moderately warm. In hot-summer regions, give plants, especially those with variegated foliage, light to medium shade. Clumps grow indefinitely without division and replanting, but you can easily extend plantings by dividing old clumps or by slicing out wedges with a spade.

Best performance is in regions that have definite winter chill and summer humidity (cool or hot). Slugs and snails are fond of hosta foliage.

HOUTTUYNIA CORDATA

Zones: 6–10 (West, except desert), 6–9 (East)
Type: Deciduous perennial
Exposure: Sun to shade
Water: Regular watering
Spacing: 18 inches

From a distance, houttuynia could be mistaken for English ivy. Heart-shaped, semiglossy leaves grow to 3 inches long, and the foliage forms an even cover to 9 inches high. The striking form 'Variegata' (sometimes sold as 'Chameleon') features splashes of cream, yellow, pink, and red on the outer portion of each leaf.

In cool-summer regions, you can grow houttuynia in sun; in all other areas, plant in light to deep shade. Plants spread by underground stems and can become somewhat invasive in the good, moist soil they prefer.

HYPERICUM CALYCINUM

AARON'S BEARD,
CREEPING ST. JOHNSWORT
Pictured on page 9

Zones: 6–10
Type: Evergreen shrub
Exposure: Sun to shade
Water: Moderate
Spacing: 18 inches

Aaron's beard is both good looking and indestructible, forming a dense, even cover to 12 inches high. Arching stems

Hosta sieboldiana

bear pairs of oval leaves to 4 inches long that are rich green in sunny locations, lighter green in shade. In late spring to early summer, nearly every stem tip bears a 3-inch yellow blossom with prominent stamens.

Plants spread aggressively by underground stems; they can be invasive in some situations, unless restricted by a barrier to control the perimeter. On the positive side, the dense mat of roots and underground stems competes easily with surface-rooted trees and helps prevent erosion on sloping ground. Any soil is suitable.

Aaron's beard is fairly drought tolerant, but it grows more attractively with at least moderate watering. Mow or shear plantings about every 3 years in late winter or early spring to renew growth and maintain an even surface.

IBERIS SEMPERVIRENS

EVERGREEN CANDYTUFT
Pictured at right

Zones: 4–10
Type: Evergreen perennial
Exposure: Sun to light shade
Water: Moderate
Spacing: 12 inches

At the peak of bloom, a planting of candytuft will be entirely white, with flattened clusters of tiny flowers completely obscuring the narrow, dark and glossy leaves. The major flowering period is early to late spring, but in mildest regions you may see flowers beginning in late fall. Each plant is a spreading hummock 8 to 12 inches high, spreading 12 to 18 inches.

Superior for ground cover use is the variety 'Snowflake', which has large flowers and foliage on a plant that spreads to 3 feet (and can be planted 18 to 24 inches apart). In warm-winter areas, it will bloom intermittently throughout the year.

After the spring flowering has finished, shear plants lightly to keep plants compact; this also encourages new growth and possible later bloom.

Iberis sempervirens

ICE PLANT

Pictured on pages 8, 17, and 56

Zones: Vary
Type: Evergreen perennials
Exposure: Sun
Water: Moderate to little
Spacing: Varies

Included under the common name "ice plant" are a number of succulent perennial plants once grouped together as *Mesembryanthemum* but now classified under different names. All have foliage that is thick and juicy, often with a powdery gray or crystalline surface. Most produce showy flowers—some almost blindingly brilliant—that resemble silky-petaled daisies; bees are attracted to the blooms.

Ice plants are not particular about soil; some of them will grow in nearly pure beach sand. Water just often enough to keep foliage from wilting or shriveling; overwatering can result in root rot or dieback, especially in heavier soils during hot weather. Fertilize lightly in mid-fall and again after flowering has finished.

Aptenia cordifolia; Zones 9 (warmest parts)–10. Succulent, bright green, inch-long leaves are heart shaped to oval; they grow on lax stems that trail to about 2 feet. Vivid purplish red, inch-wide flowers appear in spring and summer. The variety 'Variegata' has leaves margined in white. Use in small spaces, setting plants 12 to 18 inches apart.

Carpobrotus; Zones 9–10. Coarse-textured, trailing plants have thick, finger-like leaves and 2-inch, pastel blossoms. Plants will cover a considerable area on level or gently sloping ground; space new plants 18 to 24 inches apart. Avoid planting on steep banks where the weight of a rain-soaked planting could cause slippage.

C. chilensis has three-sided, straight leaves to 2 inches long; 3-inch, rosy purple flowers appear in summer. Far more common, *C. edulis* has curved leaves 4 to 5 inches long and pale yellow- to rose-colored blossoms.

Cephalophyllum 'Red Spike'; Zones 9–10. Individual plants reach 3 to 5 inches high and spread to 15 inches; bronzy red, spiky leaves point upward like slender fingers. The main display of the 2-inch, cerise red flowers comes in winter, but some bloom can occur throughout the year. Space new plants 12 inches apart; water sparingly during summer in desert areas to avoid root rot.

Delosperma; Zones vary. White trailing ice plant, *D.* 'Alba', grows in Zones 9–10. Bright green, rounded, fleshy leaves

Ice plant (Drosanthemum floribundum)

cover a low, trailing plant that roots as it spreads. Small white flowers in summer are noticeable but not showy. Space plants of this and the following two species 12 to 18 inches apart.

Protected by snow or winter mulch in the coldest regions, *D. cooperi* will grow in Zones 7–10. Plants reach 5 inches high, spreading to 2 feet, and are clothed in nearly cylindrical, fingerlike leaves. Glistening purple, 2-inch flowers appear throughout the summer.

D. nubigenum is even more cold tolerant, growing in Zones 5–10. Plants hug the ground, forming a thick carpet of cylindrical, bright green leaves that turn to glowing red in fall and remain that color until spring. Later in spring, 1- to 2-inch yellow blossoms cover the planting for about a month.

Drosanthemum; Zones 9–10 (except desert). Crystalline dots on leaves make these the most "icy" of ice plants. Rosea ice plant, *D. floribundum,* will cover large areas with a 6-inch mat of fine-textured foliage; of all the ice plants, this is the best for erosion control on steep slopes. In late spring, the planting becomes a solid sheet of cool, shimmering, light pink blossoms.

D. hispidum is a shrubbier plant, growing to 2 feet high and about 3 feet wide; it has cylindrical, inch-long leaves. Bright purple, 1-inch flowers make a fine display in late spring and early summer.

For quick cover, set plants of both species 18 inches apart.

Lampranthus; Zones 9–10 (except desert). Spreading, semishrubby plants with gray green, fingerlike leaves produce notably showy flowers from middle to late winter into spring. When planting, set plants 12 to 18 inches apart.

Brilliant orange, 2-inch flowers of *L. aurantiacus* come on bushy, compact plants to 15 inches high; variety 'Glaucus' has clear yellow flowers; those of 'Sunman' are golden yellow.

Growing to the same height but in a more spreading shape, *L. productus* has bronze-tipped foliage and inch-wide purple flowers. Trailing ice plant, *L. spectabilis,* grows to 12 inches high and produces especially showy flowers to 2½ inches across; color choices include lilac pink, rose pink, red, and purple.

Redondo creeper, *L. filicaulis,* differs in size and texture from the other three species. Thin, trailing stems and tiny leaves make a small, pink-flowered cover to 3 inches high. Plants spread slowly and grow best in small areas.

Malephora; Zones 9–10. Gray green, slender fingers of foliage form a dense backdrop to bright blossoms; the main flowering occurs in spring, but additional blooms appear throughout the year. Space new plants 12 to 18 inches apart.

Lower growing (to 6 inches) and trailing, *M. crocea* features 1½-inch flowers of red-shaded yellow. *M. c. purpureocrocea* has salmon pink blossoms that harmonize with bluish green leaves; it can be used to control erosion on moderately steep land. *M. luteola,* a more compact plant that grows to 12 inches high, has gray green leaves and small yellow flowers.

JASMINUM POLYANTHUM

Zones: 8–10
Type: Evergreen woody vine
Exposure: Sun
Water: Regular watering
Spacing: 10 feet

Of the true jasmines that have fragrant flowers, this is the best species for ground cover use. (For the plant called star jasmine, see *Trachelospermum jasminoides,* page 76.) Twining stems reach out vigorously to 20 feet and bear leaves composed of five to seven narrow leaflets; the plant sheds some of its leaves in colder winter areas.

Clusters of deliciously scented, star-shaped flowers appear over an extended period—from late winter to midsummer in mild regions, mid-spring to midsummer elsewhere. Petal surfaces are white and backs are pink, giving flowers a rosy suffusion.

Plantings may become a bit tangled as stems twine among one another. When this occurs, thin out or cut back entangled growth before flowering begins.

JUNIPERUS

JUNIPER

*Pictured at right and on
pages 10, 16, 30, and 58*

Zones: Vary
Type: Evergreen shrubs
Exposure: Sun to partial shade
Water: Moderate
Spacing: 5 to 6 feet

Junipers are the universal (and seemingly ubiquitous) ground cover. You can find junipers that will flourish in the range of climates extending from Maine to California and from Minnesota to Florida. Eight species furnish prostrate forms for use as ground covers; available varieties are numerous, with new ones entering the nursery trade almost every year.

The lists below, grouped by species, highlight the most widely sold, proven kinds. Nurseries in your area may carry less well known but equally desirable varieties.

Juniper foliage is of two kinds: juvenile leaves are short, spiky needles; mature leaves are tiny, overlapping scales. Some varieties may bear only juvenile foliage, some only mature foliage, and others a combination of the two. Foliage colors range from silvery blue through many shades of green to yellowish green and variegated. Junipers are coniferous plants, allied to pine, fir, and spruce; but instead of bearing cones, junipers produce blue to black, berrylike "fruits."

One of juniper's strong points is its adaptability: plants will thrive in climates ranging from cool to hot, moist to dry, and in soils from light to heavy, acid to alkaline. But all are intolerant on one point: waterlogged soil, which can lead to root rot and plant death.

In many situations, junipers rate as drought tolerant. Where summers are cool to moderately warm, junipers growing in loam to claylike soils may need little or no summer watering. In hot-summer areas, moderate watering will see them through the dry season.

Where summer is hot, especially hot and dry, give a juniper planting partial shade. In cooler regions, plants will accept a bit of shade, but they will grow better in full sun.

Juniperus horizontalis 'Douglasii'

Even though junipers increase at a slow to moderate pace, you should space new plants 5 to 6 feet apart to avoid future overcrowding. Mulch well between plants to keep weeds under control. For seasonal interest during the early years, you can plant annuals in open soil between juniper plants. You'll achieve a faster cover by planting junipers 3 to 4 feet apart; but when they begin to crowd, remove every other plant.

The listing below describes the eight species and the most popular varieties of each.

Juniperus chinensis; Zones 4–10. *J. c. procumbens,* Japanese garden juniper, produces blue green, feathery foliage on a plant to 3 feet high, spreading 12 to 20 feet. Its variety 'Nana' has shorter needles on a plant to 1 foot high and 4 to 5 feet across.

J. c. 'San Jose' has both needlelike and scalelike foliage in dark sage green; plants grow to 2 feet high and 6 or more feet across.

Sargent juniper or Shimpaku, *J. c. sargentii,* has gray green, feathery foliage on a ground-hugging plant to 1 foot high and 10 feet across. Variety 'Glauca' has

blue green foliage; that of 'Viridis' is bright green.

Juniperus communis; Zones 2–9. *J. c. saxatilis* reaches 1 foot high, trailing to 6 to 8 feet, with gray to gray green foliage; secondary branches point upward from prostrate main limbs.

Juniperus conferta; Zones 5–10. The shore juniper features soft, bright green needles on a trailing plant to 8 feet across and 1 foot high. Although native to a cool, moist climate, it will grow in dry, hot-summer regions if given well-drained soil and regular watering. Selected varieties include 'Emerald Sea' and heat-tolerant 'Blue Pacific' with blue green leaves.

Juniperus horizontalis; Zones vary. Two varieties will grow in Zones 4–10. Waukegan juniper, *J. h.* 'Douglasii', trails to 10 feet but rises no more than 1 foot

Juniperus borizontalis 'Wiltonii'

high; rich green new growth becomes steel blue, then turns plum color in winter.

Andorra juniper, *J. b.* 'Plumosa', has gray green foliage that also turns plum color in winter. Main limbs spread to 10 feet, the secondary branches growing upward to 1½ feet.

Three *J. borizontalis* varieties will grow in Zones 5–10. *J. b.* 'Bar Harbor' spreads quickly to 10 feet but grows no more than a foot high; its feathery foliage is blue gray, turning plum color in winter. As the plant ages, the foliage dies back in the center, exposing the main limbs.

With dense, gray green foliage, *J. b.* 'Blue Mat' is more compact—6 to 7 feet across and no more than 12 inches high. Varieties 'Emerald Spreader' and 'Turquoise Spreader' are low (about 6 inches), dense, and feathery, spreading only 4 to 6 feet; the foliage of the former is bright green, that of the latter a more bluish shade.

Blue carpet juniper—*J. b.* 'Wiltonii', sometimes sold as *J. b.* 'Blue Rug'—forms long, trailing main branches with secondary stems rising no higher than 4 inches; color is a striking silver blue.

Juniperus sabina; Zones 4–10, with one exception. *J. s.* 'Blue Danube' is almost shrubby, spreading its lacy, blue green foliage to about 5 feet while rising to around 18 inches. Bright green *J. s.* 'Arcadia' has a similarly lacy apppearance but grows to 12 inches high, spreading to 10 feet.

J. s. 'Broadmoor' carries soft, bright green foliage on a dense, mounding plant to a bit more than a foot high and 10 feet wide. Slightly lower but also with soft green foliage, *J. s.* 'Calgary Carpet' will succeed in colder Zone 3.

J. s. 'Buffalo' offers feathery, bright green foliage on a plant that spreads only to 8 feet, rising no more than 12 inches. *J. s.* 'Scandia' presents fresh, bright green, lacy foliage on a compact plant to 8 feet across and a foot high.

Tamarix, or "Tam", juniper, *J. s.* 'Tamariscifolia' is an old favorite with the widest spread—to 20 feet; dense sprays of blue green foliage rise to 18 inches.

Juniperus scopulorum; Zones 4–10. The Rocky Mountain juniper has several prostrate forms, one of the best of which is *J. s.* 'White's Silver King'. Scalelike leaves are pale, silvery blue on a dense plant less than a foot high but spreading 6 to 8 feet. *J. s.* 'Blue Creeper' is similar but a bit less silvery and taller (to 2 feet).

Juniperus squamata; Zones 4–10. Slow-growing *J. s.* 'Blue Carpet' reaches a foot high and 5 feet across, with bright, blue gray foliage.

Juniperus virginiana; Zones 3–10. Fine-textured, feathery *J. v.* 'Silver Spreader' features silvery green foliage on an 18-inch plant with a 6- to 8-foot spread. Because this species is an alternate host for cedar-apple rust, it should not be planted in regions where apples are an important home or commercial crop.

LAMIUM MACULATUM

DEAD NETTLE
Pictured on page 11

Zones: 5–10
Type: Evergreen to deciduous perennial
Exposure: Shade
Water: Regular watering
Spacing: 18 to 24 inches

Varieties of dead nettle are suitable plants for brightening shaded situations. Prominently veined, heart-shaped leaves to 2 inches long are furry to the touch; sprawling stems root as they spread. Foliage mass reaches about 6 inches high. Small, hooded flowers (usually pink) bloom on short spikes in late spring or early summer.

Most widely sold are forms with variegated foliage. 'Variegatum' has dark green leaves with a silvery white stripe along the midrib of each. 'Beacon Silver' is almost totally silvery gray; only its leaf margins are green. 'White Nancy' is virtually identical except for its white flowers.

Similar to the dead nettles, but a larger plant, is the yellow archangel,

Lamiastrum galeobdolon. Its 3-inch leaves rise to 12 inches high; flowers are yellow. The variety 'Variegatum' has dark green leaves marbled with white.

LANTANA

Pictured on page 60

Zones: 9 (warmest parts)–10
Type: Evergreen shrubby vine
Exposure: Sun
Water: Moderate
Spacing: 3 feet

Where frost is rare or light, reliable, easy-to-grow lantanas provide color for most of the year. Small, individual flowers are packed into nosegaylike clusters about 1½ inches in diameter, borne atop dark green foliage with a crinkled, sandpaper texture.

The most familiar ground cover type is *L. montevidensis* (*L. sellowiana*), with lavender flowers on a wide-spreading plant that may reach 1 to 1½ feet high. It has been a parent (paired with a shrubby species) of numerous colorful hybrids, some of which have inherited its spreading habit.

The following varieties may reach 2 to 3 feet high, spreading to 6 to 8 feet: 'Confetti' (flowers of yellow, pink, and purple), 'Cream Carpet' (cream and yellow), 'Pink Frolic' (pink and yellow), 'Spreading Sunset' (orange red), 'Spreading Sunshine' (yellow), 'Sunburst' (golden yellow), and 'Tangerine' (orange).

Growing to about 2 feet high and spreading to 6 feet are 'Gold Mound' (yellow orange) and 'Kathleen' (pink and gold).

Lantanas have no soil preference and need only infrequent, deep watering. They're especially effective on sunny slopes, where they help control erosion. In early spring, cut out dead branches and old, woody stems to keep plantings low and well foliaged.

LAURENTIA FLUVIATILIS

BLUE STAR CREEPER
Pictured below and on pages 3 and 14

Zones: 8–10 (West, except desert)
Type: Evergreen perennial
Exposure: Sun to light shade
Water: Regular watering
Spacing: 6 to 12 inches

With its tiny, bright green leaves and ground-hugging habit, blue star creeper gives the effect of moss as it blankets the soil, flows around rocks, or fills in between paving stones. But in unmosslike fashion, it has star-shaped, light blue blossoms (about the size of a pencil eraser) scattered over its surface in late spring and summer. Nurseries often sell it as *Isotoma fluviatilis.*

Where summers are hot, plant in light shade. For best appearance, water blue star creeper regularly and give it a light application of fertilizer monthly during spring, summer, and into fall.

Laurentia fluviatilis

LIRIOPE

LILY TURF

Zones: Vary
Type: Evergreen perennial
Exposure: Sun to shade
Water: Regular watering
Spacing: 8 to 12 inches

You can't walk on this "turf," but you can enjoy the illusion of coarse, shaggy grass with the bonus of attractive summer flowers that resemble grape hyacinth (*Muscari*).

Very narrow, strap-shaped leaves form thick clumps of arching foliage. It makes a particularly effective transition planting between lawn and trees or high shrubbery. Lily turfs are frequently used in Oriental-inspired landscapes. Two available species (and several varieties) give you a choice of heights.

Creeping lily turf, *L. spicata,* is the lower-growing species. Rather lax, dark green foliage rises to about 9 inches; clumps spread by underground stems to solidly colonize an area. Spikes of pale lavender to white flowers barely appear through the leaves. Variety 'Silver Dragon' has leaves striped in white.

Big blue lily turf, *L. muscari,* has stiffer but still arching foliage that can reach to 1½ feet. The plants form large clumps that don't spread. Typically, flowers are dark violet, borne on spikes rising above the foliage mass.

A number of varieties are available in nurseries (particularly in the southeastern United States). 'Lilac Beauty' has pale violet flowers. 'Majestic' carries its dark violet blooms in flattened, cockscomblike clusters. 'Silvery Sunproof' has more distinctly upright foliage, each leaf striped gold that ages to white; showy flowers are lavender.

New leaves of 'Variegata' (sometimes sold as *Ophiopogon jaburan* 'Variegata') are yellow edged during their first year, turning dark green thereafter; its violet blossoms are much darker than those of 'Silvery Sunproof'.

All lily turfs need well-drained soil; they look best with regular watering,

Lantana montevidensis

even though they will persist with some drought. Where summers are mild, you can plant in sun or shade; hot-summer regions call for at least partial or light shade (*L. m.* 'Variegata' is always best with some shade).

Plantings need some tidying up in late winter or early spring. Before new growth begins, mow or shear *L. spicata* plantings to get rid of shabby old leaves. With *L. muscari* and varieties, cut back brown and tired old leaves after new growth has started. Slugs and snails may require control.

LONICERA

HONEYSUCKLE
Pictured on facing page

Zones: 5–10
Type: Evergreen to deciduous woody vine; semi-evergreen shrub
Exposure: Sun to partial shade
Water: Moderate
Spacing: Varies

Two quite different honeysuckles can do service as ground covers. The first is

Hall's honeysuckle, *L. japonica* 'Halliana', an aggressively vigorous, twining vine that will quickly cover a large surface area if there's nothing for it to climb. Stems feature 3-inch, oval, deep green leaves in opposite pairs—evergreen in mild-winter zones, semi-evergreen to deciduous in progressively colder areas.

Notably fragrant flowers are tubular, flaring out to unequal petals, initially white but aging to yellow; season begins in late spring and lasts into summer.

Best uses are to cover slopes, control erosion, and blanket large expanses where the plant's vigor won't engulf other plants. Space plants 3 to 5 feet apart. Shear or mow plantings nearly to ground level annually in late winter; this prevents the buildup of dead stems that can be a fire hazard if allowed to accumulate.

The goldnet honeysuckle, *L. j.* 'Aureoreticulata', is less rampant and offers lighter green leaves prominently veined in yellow.

The second species is semi-evergreen privet honeysuckle, *L. pileata,* which is, by contrast, a spreading shrub 2 to 3 feet high; its stiffly horizontal branches are clothed in 1½-inch, oval leaves. Sweetly fragrant, small white flowers in mid-spring are followed by small purple berries.

Spaced 2 feet apart, plants form a neat, noninvasive cover for slopes or flat areas. They thrive in full sun in coastal gardens but prefer partial or light shade in hotter, drier climates. Performance is not satisfactory in the desert.

LOTUS

Zones: Vary
Type: Evergreen, deciduous perennials
Exposure: Sun
Water: Varies
Spacing: Varies

The two *Lotus* species used as ground covers differ markedly in appearance and garden use. Parrot's beak, *L. berthelotii,* is less cold tolerant (Zone 10 and warmer parts of Zone 9, but not desert) and is the showier of the two. Creeping stems with feathery, silver gray leaves form a soft-appearing carpet upon which float narrow-petalled, inch-long scarlet blossoms in early to midsummer.

Set 2 feet apart, plants will soon fill in; at the top of a retaining wall, foliage will spill over in a filmy curtain. Plants need well-drained soil and moderate watering; cut back occasionally to keep plants bushy.

Bird's-foot trefoil, *L. corniculatus,* grows in Zones 5–10; it becomes totally dormant in all but the warmest-winter regions. It excels as a lawn substitute (even with a bit of foot traffic), where it resembles a thick mat of clover. Dark green leaves contain three small leaflets in clover fashion; clusters of small yellow flowers resembling sweet peas appear in summer and fall. Its common name comes from the slender seed capsules that radiate from atop the flower stalks like the feet of a bird.

For a quick "lawn," sow seeds on ground prepared as for a turf lawn. Or set out plants 6 inches apart. Water regularly during the warm days of spring, summer, and early fall for a lush, lawnlike appearance. Once established, plantings need only moderate watering.

Occasionally mow lawn-substitute plantings to 2 inches to maintain an even surface. Plantings will regrow from the roots each year; new plants will germinate from seed.

LYSIMACHIA NUMMULARIA

MONEYWORT, CREEPING JENNY

Zones: 3–10 (except desert)
Type: Evergreen perennial
Exposure: Shade
Water: Regular watering
Spacing: 12 to 18 inches

A bit of shade and moist soil are all that moneywort needs to become a lush, low carpet of light green. In fact, it thrives in continually damp soil that will defeat most other ground covers.

Leaves are nearly round, less than an inch across, on rapidly spreading stems that root where leaf nodes contact soil. The variety 'Aurea' has yellow foliage. Summer brings a display of inch-wide, bright yellow flowers.

Lonicera japonica 'Halliana'

MAHONIA

Pictured below

Zones: 5–9 (West), 5–8 (East)
Type: Evergreen shrubs
Exposure: Varies
Water: Moderate to little
Spacing: 24 inches

The various mahonias are neat, tailored shrubs that retain their good looks throughout the year. Each leaf consists of oval leaflets with spiny, hollylike margins. Showy clusters of small, cup-shaped yellow flowers appear at branch tips in spring, followed by blue, pea-size berries. Plants spread at a moderate rate by underground stems.

Compact Oregon grape, *M. aquifolium* 'Compacta', is the most widely available. Leaves have from five to nine glossy, 3-inch-long leaflets; new growth emerges a bright copper color. Plantings, which may reach 2 feet high, grow best in partial to light shade where summer is hot.

Longleaf mahonia, *M. nervosa,* has as many as 21 glossy leaflets to nearly 4 inches long, with leaves clustered toward the branch tips. Plants generally remain about 2 feet high; cut back any tall stems to keep the planting even. For best appearance, plant in partial to light shade in all zones (it is not successful, though, in the desert). In cool-summer areas, it will grow very compactly in full sun.

Creeping mahonia, *M. repens,* reaches about 3 feet high. It bears dull, blue green leaflets to 2½ inches long that become bronze colored in winter. Plants will take full sun (except in desert gardens) as well as light shade.

Mahonia nervosa

MAZUS REPTANS

Pictured on facing page

Zones: 4–10 (except desert)
Type: Evergreen to deciduous perennial
Exposure: Sun to light shade
Water: Regular watering
Spacing: 6 to 12 inches

All aspects of this ground cover are small, but in this case "small" does not mean fragile. Creeping stems root along the ground, bearing light green, narrow leaves to an inch long on branches no more than 2 inches high. From spring into summer, plantings are dotted with small clusters of lobelialike flowers in dark lavender spotted with yellow and white.

If given good soil and ample water, dense, ground-hugging growth will quickly fill in between paving stones, flow among rocks, and solidly cover small areas. Plantings will even take light foot traffic. Evergreen in Zones 9–10, the plants die to the ground over winter in colder zones but will regrow in spring.

MENTHA REQUIENII

JEWEL MINT OF CORSICA

Zones: 7–10
Type: Evergreen perennial
Exposure: Sun to light shade
Water: Regular watering
Spacing: 6 to 12 inches

This ground cover invites foot traffic: when crushed, its leaves emit a pleasant minty or sagelike fragrance.

Creeping stems, which grow less than an inch high, bear tiny, round, bright green leaves and, in summer, equally small, light purple flowers. The moss-like effect is attractive in small areas—between paving stones, on earth steps, and alongside natural-earth pathways, for example.

In Zones 7, 8, and colder parts of 9, plants will freeze to the ground during winter but regrow in spring.

MYOPORUM PARVIFOLIUM

Zones: 9–10 (West, except desert)
Type: Evergreen shrub
Exposure: Sun
Water: Moderate
Spacing: 5 feet

Where coastal conditions influence the climate, gardeners value myoporum for ease of growth and attractive appearance the year around. Gardeners in hotter inland climates can derive the same satisfaction from the heat-tolerant variety 'Putah Creek'.

Leaves are narrow and thick, to an inch long, densely covering the trailing branches that root where they touch soil. Bell-shaped, white, ½-inch summer flowers are followed by small purple berries. The basic species grows 3 to 6 inches high; 'Putah Creek' may reach 1 foot.

A hybrid plant, *M.* 'Pacificum', grows especially fast, rising to 2 feet high and spreading to 30 feet. Space plants 12 to 15 feet apart.

Myoporum is a fine choice for planting on slopes and to control erosion, due to its fast, low, dense growth and multitude of roots from spreading stems. Plants need well-drained soil; in some beach communities, they thrive in nearly pure sand.

Near the coast, plants tolerate some drought but look better with periodic watering during summer. In hotter inland areas, give plantings moderate watering during the warmest months.

MYOSOTIS SCORPIOIDES

FORGET-ME-NOT

Zones: 4–10
Type: Deciduous perennial
Exposure: Shade
Water: Regular watering
Spacing: 6 to 12 inches

Forget-me-not's small flowers of purest light blue illuminate shaded and woodland gardens with an azure haze in spring and summer. Borne in elongated, curving clusters, blooms rise above spreading plants with narrow, bright green, 2-inch

Mazus reptans

leaves. Plants grow 6 to 12 inches high, spreading by creeping roots.

Forget-me-not will persist for years when given ample moisture and soil amended with organic matter. In colder zones, plants die to the ground over winter and regrow in spring.

NANDINA DOMESTICA

HEAVENLY BAMBOO

Zones: 8–10 (West), 8–9 (East)
Type: Evergreen shrub
Exposure: Sun to light shade
Water: Regular to moderate
Spacing: 12 to 18 inches

Nurseries offer several low-growing or dwarf varieties of the normally 6- to 8-foot-high heavenly bamboo. Of those,

'Harbour Dwarf' is the best ground cover, spreading at a moderate rate from underground stems. Plants grow 1½ to 2 feet high but have all the feathery grace of the basic species.

Upright stems carry leaves almost parallel to the ground, each leaf containing numerous narrow, pointed leaflets in groups of three. New growth in spring is pinkish green; in fall, cold weather turns leaves to shades of orange to bronze.

Best winter foliage color comes on plants growing in full sun, although in desert gardens and in hot-summer western valleys, light or partial shade is necessary. Chlorotic foliage may be a problem where soil is alkaline; treat the problem with iron chelate or iron sulfate.

Nepeta faassenii

its need is moderate. After blossoming is finished, shear off faded flower spikes to encourage a later flowering. Before new growth starts in late winter or early spring, cut back or shear plants by about half; new growth will fill in quickly.

OPHIOPOGON JAPONICUS

MONDO GRASS
Pictured on page 11

Zones: 8–10
Type: Evergreen perennial
Exposure: Sun to shade
Water: Regular watering
Spacing: 6 to 8 inches

This close relative of *Liriope* (see page 60) is even more grasslike than that plant. Dense clumps consist of lax, dark green leaves ⅛ inch wide and 8 to 12 inches long. Plants spread slowly by underground stems to form a solid, shaggy "turf" that rises 6 to 8 inches high.

Small, pale lavender flowers appear in summer on short spikes that are largely hidden among the leaves; round, pea-size blue fruits form after flowers fade. The variety 'Nana' ('Kyoto Dwarf') grows to about half the size of the basic species.

Plant mondo grass in well-drained soil. In cool-summer areas, you can plant in full sun; elsewhere, locate plantings in partial or light shade. Plants are somewhat drought tolerant, but water regularly for best appearance.

If the plants become shabby looking from an accumulation of old, dead foliage, you can mow or cut back in early spring before new growth begins.

NEPETA FAASSENII

CATMINT
Pictured above

Zones: 4–10 (West), 4–9 (East)
Type: Evergreen to deciduous perennial
Exposure: Sun
Water: Moderate
Spacing: 18 inches

A favorite foreground plant for perennial borders and herb gardens, catmint also serves well as a small-scale ground cover, providing a note of coolness to the late spring and early summer landscape.

Plants reach 6 to 8 inches high and spread to about 3 feet in diameter; catmint's many thin stems are set with small, oval, deeply veined, gray green leaves.

Loose clusters of ½-inch, lavender blue flowers rise 12 to 18 inches, creating a bluish cloud over the planting. The common name tells you that cats find this plant attractive, although not as enticing as the related catnip (*N. cataria*).

Catmint needs well-drained soil; it will accept regular watering, even though

OSTEOSPERMUM FRUTICOSUM

TRAILING AFRICAN DAISY
Pictured on facing page

Zones: 9–10 (West, except desert)
Type: Evergreen perennial
Exposure: Sun
Water: Moderate
Spacing: 2 feet

Trailing African daisy will bloom on sunny days throughout the year, but its

Osteospermum fruticosum

main flowering period begins in mid-fall and continues through winter; thus, when garden color is usually at its lowest ebb, these plantings will be covered by a sheet of flowers.

Each blossom is a purple-centered, 2- to 3-inch daisy; lavender petals fade to white but remain purple on their undersides. Nurseries may also offer several pure white and solid purple varieties.

Oval, gray green leaves 1 to 4 inches long cover fast-growing plants that root along stems as they spread. Each plant may grow to 4 feet in diameter in a year, rising to a height of 6 to 12 inches.

Trailing African daisy prospers both at the seashore and in hot-summer inland areas, but it does not grow well in the desert. Although they will tolerate drought, established plants look better with moderate watering in good, well-drained soil. With regular watering, a large planting can help retard fire.

When old plantings become untidy, cut back to healthy new growth after the main flowering period.

PACHYSANDRA TERMINALIS

JAPANESE SPURGE

Zones: 4–9 (except desert)
Type: Evergreen shrub
Exposure: Shade
Water: Regular watering
Spacing: 12 inches

Japanese spurge brings a touch of elegance to shade gardens. Foliage forms an even carpet about 10 inches high (lower in light shade) of lustrous, oval leaves carried in whorls toward the ends of upright stems.

In late spring or early summer, spikes of tiny, fluffy white flowers appear at stem tips; small white fruits often follow. Variety 'Variegata' has white leaf margins; use it to add extra sparkle to heavy shade.

Plants spread at a moderate rate by underground stems, even competing well with shallow-rooted trees. They grow best in good, somewhat acid soil with an annual fertilizer application in early spring.

PARTHENOCISSUS QUINQUEFOLIA

VIRGINIA CREEPER

Zones: 3–10
Type: Deciduous woody vine
Exposure: Sun to light shade
Water: Regular watering
Spacing: 3 feet

Gardeners in eastern North America know Virginia creeper as a rampant, scrambling vine renowned for its annual display of brilliant foliage. Glossy green in spring and summer, leaves turn blazing orange to red early in fall.

Each leaf contains five separate, oval leaflets to 6 inches long with distinct veins and sawtooth edges. Leaves are widely spaced along stems, providing a loose rather than dense cover. Variety 'Englemannii' has smaller and more closely spaced leaves.

Inconspicuous clusters of tiny flowers are followed by small, dark blue fruits. Stems easily cover flat ground or sloping land, rooting where they contact moist soil. When they encounter a vertical surface—tree trunk, fence, or shrubbery—they'll climb quickly, holding fast with clinging tendrils.

PAXISTIMA

Zones: 5–9 (except desert)
Type: Evergreen shrubs
Exposure: Sun to partial shade
Water: Regular watering
Spacing: 12 to 18 inches

Two North American species offer glossy, narrow foliage on dense, compact plants. They make good fillers or borders when used with showier large shrubs or in woodland settings.

The smaller of the two is *P. canbyi,* which grows at a slow to moderate rate to 12 inches high; the leaves, about an inch long and ¼ inch wide, become bronzy in the chill of fall and winter.

Oregon boxwood, *P. myrsinites,* has larger leaves and may reach 2 or more feet in height, especially in shaded locations; it can be kept low with periodic pruning.

Both species will grow in full sun where summers are cool or moderate, but they also thrive in light or partial shade. Some shade is necessary in hot-summer regions. Plant in well-drained soil that is somewhat acid.

PELARGONIUM PELTATUM

IVY GERANIUM
Pictured at left and on page 16

Zones: 9 (warmest parts)–10
Type: Evergreen shrubby perennial
Exposure: Sun
Water: Moderate
Spacing: 18 to 24 inches

Where frost is light or rare, ivy geranium is virtually unbeatable for providing plenty of color over a long period of time with minimal care.

Glossy, five-lobed leaves 2 to 3 inches across resemble the foliage of English ivy (*Hedera helix,* page 51), but they're thick and succulent. Trailing stems grow fairly rapidly, in time building up to about 12 inches high.

Individual flowers are single or double, about an inch across, in rounded clusters of five to ten. Flowering is heaviest from mid-spring to mid-fall but can occur the year around in frostless areas. Flower colors range from white, lavender, and pink shades to magenta and red; you can also find striped combinations.

Nurseries may sell named varieties or may offer plants labeled only as to color. Plants of seed-grown Summer Showers

Pelargonium peltatum

strain come in mixed colors. Specialist growers and some nurseries offer varieties with variegated foliage.

Ivy geraniums prefer well-drained or sandy soil; if soil is alkaline, add acid amendments such as redwood bark or peat moss. Water only when the upper inch of soil is dry.

Plants in reasonably good soil may not need fertilizer or, at most, only one application in late winter or early spring. Fertilize plants in sandy soil two or three times during the growing season.

PHLOX SUBULATA

MOSS PINK
Pictured at right and on page 5

Zones: 4–9
Type: Evergreen perennial
Exposure: Sun
Water: Moderate
Spacing: 12 to 18 inches

Moss pink is a favorite border and rock garden plant; the spreading, 6-inch-high plants are entirely covered with blossoms during the month-long season in late spring to early summer. Planted in mass as a ground cover, they'll form an arresting floral carpet.

Each flower is circular, to ¾ inch across; colors include white, pink shades, red, violet, and lavender blue. Nurseries sell plants labeled by color, or they may offer superior named varieties.

Creeping stems form dense mats of needlelike leaves to ½ inch long.

Plants thrive in well-drained soil with moderate watering. To encourage dense new growth, cut back or shear plants by about half after flowering has finished.

PHYLA NODIFLORA

LIPPIA
Pictured on page 68

Zones: 9–10
Type: Evergreen perennial
Exposure: Sun
Water: Regular to moderate
Spacing: 12 to 24 inches

Even though its appearance is not at all grasslike, lippia's ground-hugging growth

Phlox subulata

and ability to endure foot traffic have established its use as a lawn substitute. Creeping stems bear oval, grayish green leaves to ¾ inch long; in full sun this "turf" reaches no higher than 2 inches.

Tiny lavender to pink flowers clustered in rounded, ½-inch heads appear from spring to fall. The blossoms attract bees; to avoid this problem, mow periodically to remove flowers.

Lippia grows well in a wide range of soils. You can set established clumps 2 feet apart or plant rooted sprigs at 12-inch intervals. Plants perform well in desert gardens, although susceptibility to nematodes hampers growth in areas where soils are infested.

Appearance is unattractive during the winter dormant period. Fertilize plants in early spring to encourage fresh new growth.

POLYGONUM

KNOTWEED

Zones: Vary
Type: Evergreen, deciduous perennials
Exposure: Sun to light shade
Water: Moderate
Spacing: Varies

Used where their invasive growth won't infiltrate other plantings, the knotweeds serve well as good-looking, low-maintenance ground covers.

Lower growing of the two species is evergreen *P. capitatum,* which forms a thick, spreading cover to 6 inches high. The 1½-inch, oval leaves are dark green when new but become tinged with pink as they age, combining well with the cloverlike heads of pink flowers (carried on

Phyla nodiflora

POTENTILLA

CINQUEFOIL
Pictured on facing page and page 30

Zones: 4–9 (West), 4–8 (East)
Type: Evergreen perennials
Exposure: Sun to light shade
Water: Moderate
Spacing: 12 inches

Growth habit and general appearance suggest strawberry (see *Fragaria chiloensis,* page 47), but each cinquefoil leaf contains five leaflets (as the name suggests) instead of the strawberry's three. In spring and early summer, small yellow flowers that resemble single roses dot the foliage cover.

Both species described below prefer average soil, moderate watering, and full sun (except where summer is hot).

Foliage color easily distinguishes *P. cinerea:* each wedge-shaped leaflet is gray and hairy, with a white, woolly underside. Half-inch, pale yellow flowers nestle against the leaves; spreading, matted stems grow at a moderate rate to build a foliage mass 4 inches high.

In contrast, spring cinquefoil, *P. tabernaemontanii* (sometimes sold as *P. verna*), has glossy green leaflets and butter yellow blossoms. Growth is more rapid, building to 6 inches high; if you wish, mow occasionally to even up the surface.

PRATIA ANGULATA

Zones: 7–10
Type: Evergreen perennial
Exposure: Sun to shade
Water: Regular watering
Spacing: 6 to 8 inches

Pratia's dense, lush carpet of foliage has the succulent greenness of baby's tears (*Soleirolia soleirolii,* page 74), combined with rounded, ½-inch leaves similar to those of dichondra. Creeping stems spread at a moderate rate, rooting at the joints, to form a glossy, dark green mat. White or blue white summer flowers resemble the related *Lobelia.*

pink stems) that are present throughout the warmer months.

Foliage will be damaged or killed at 28°F/-2°C, but roots will survive into Zone 8 temperatures. Plants seed themselves freely and will grow as an annual ground cover in colder regions. Set plants 12 inches apart in sun or shade; water regularly for best appearance.

Deciduous *P. cuspidatum compactum* (often sold as *P. reynoutria*) is taller (10 to 24 inches high) and will grow in Zones 4–10. Wiry, red, upright stems bear light green, red-veined leaves; these are lance to heart shaped and 3 to 6 inches long. Small, light pink flowers in fluffy heads open from red buds in late summer. Foliage turns bright red in fall; then the entire plant dies back to the ground.

This species, which spreads by underground stems, is a good choice for controlling erosion on sunny hillsides that receive little water. Set plants 2 feet apart and water moderately until established; thereafter, give moderate to little water.

Give pratia good soil and ample water. Where summers are cool, you can plant in sun; in warm to hot regions, locate plantings in light or partial shade. Despite its perishable appearance, pratia will grow in the desert when its cultural needs are met.

PYRACANTHA

FIRETHORN

Zones: Vary
Type: Evergreen shrubs
Exposure: Sun
Water: Moderate
Spacing: Varies

The large, shrubby firethorns are a staple of the nursery trade; they're widely planted for their springtime show of small, fragrant white flowers and striking fall display of orange to red, pea-size berries.

A number of prostrate, low, and spreading varieties, available for ground cover use, provide the same seasonal interest. All have small, glossy, oval leaves and grow at a moderate to rapid rate. The needlelike thorns make firethorn an effective barrier plant.

Three firethorns will grow in Zones 7–10. Orange-fruited *P. angustifolia* 'Gnome' has dense foliage on a spreading, nearly prostrate plant; space individual plants 3 feet apart. *P. coccinea* 'Lowboy', with similar growth and orange fruits, is the best choice for the coldest parts of Zone 7.

For red fruits, look for *P.* 'Walderi' (sometimes sold as *P.* 'Walderi Prostrata'). Growth is wide spreading, to 1½ feet high; plant 4 to 5 feet apart.

Gardeners in Zones 8–10 can consider two additional varieties. *P.* 'Ruby Mound' is well described by its name— bright red fruits appear on rounded, spreading plants that reach about 1½ feet high and 3 feet wide; set plants 2 feet apart. Red-fruited *P.* 'Santa Cruz' (*P.* 'Santa Cruz Prostrata') is spreading rather than mounding and easily kept below 3 feet high; plant 4 to 5 feet apart.

All firethorns are easy to grow but are susceptible to pests. Scale, spider mites, and woolly aphids may be problems.

Fireblight, which kills branches, leaving them blackened and sooty appearing, may appear following a moist spring. Cut out infected branches 4 to 6 inches below the obvious infection. If you make more than one cut, disinfect shears between cuts for 20 to 30 seconds with rubbing alcohol or a 10 percent solution of household bleach.

RANUNCULUS REPENS 'PLENIFLORUS'

CREEPING BUTTERCUP

Zones: 4–9
Type: Deciduous perennial
Exposure: Shade
Water: Regular watering
Spacing: 12 to 18 inches

In shaded situations with moist soil, creeping buttercup is a rapidly spreading ground cover; stems root at the joints. Plants will invade other plantings, or even spread into a lawn, if not checked periodically.

Long-stalked, glossy, rounded leaves are deeply cut into numerous segments; foliage cover is dense and about 12

Potentilla tabernaemontanii

inches high. In spring, button-shaped, double yellow flowers rise above foliage on 1- to 2-foot stems.

The basic species, *R. repens,* has showy, single yellow flowers. Plants spread more aggressively than those of the double variety.

RIBES VIBURNIFOLIUM

CATALINA PERFUME, EVERGREEN CURRANT

Zones: 9–10 (West, except desert)
Type: Evergreen shrub
Exposure: Sun to shade
Water: Moderate to little
Spacing: 3 feet

Rosa 'Etain'

Catalina perfume is chiefly valued for its ability to thrive in shaded locations that receive little water, although it will also grow in sunny situations in coastal gardens. The low, scrambling shrub has reddish brown stems that root wherever they contact moist soil.

Rounded, 1-inch leaves of lustrous dark green appear attractively fresh and clean even during the heat and dryness of summer. Foliage is pleasantly aromatic after a rainfall or when crushed. Short, upright clusters of small, light pink to purplish flowers appear from late winter to mid-spring; small red berries often follow.

Widely spreading plants may reach 3 feet high but can be kept lower with judicious pruning.

ROSA

ROSE
Pictured below

Zones: 6–10 (except where noted)
Type: Evergreen to deciduous shrubs
Exposure: Sun
Water: Regular watering
Spacing: 8 to 10 feet

A number of diverse climbing roses have traditionally been used as ground covers, some of them naturally sprawling, others with canes limber enough to be pinned to the ground. Most of these were roses that flowered only in spring—many of them hybrids of *R. wichuraiana,* described below.

In recent years, rose breeders have sought to develop roses that could serve as ground covers and flower repeatedly during the warm months. All the roses described below, except as noted, will blossom from spring through summer and into fall, climate permitting.

Roses grow most vigorously in good soil with regular watering. Unlike ordinary bush roses, these ground covers won't need an annual pruning, but they should be thinned of old, unproductive, and dead wood every so often.

Apply fertilizer in late winter or early spring. One attribute of a first-rate ground cover rose is its resistance to foliage diseases; however, various pest controls may be needed from time to time.

'Etain'. This has the glossy leaves and lax canes of a wichuraiana rambler, but the plant flowers repeatedly throughout the season. From apricot pink buds come 3-inch, pale pink blossoms in clusters.

'Fiona'. Small, semidouble, rich dark red blossoms appear on a spreading, moderate-size plant with small, semiglossy foliage.

'Max Graf'. This once-blooming hybrid of *R. wichuraiana* (below) features large, single pink flowers. Plant has trailing stems with especially handsome, glossy foliage.

'Mermaid'; Zones 8–10. This very large-growing, shrubby climber with evergreen, glossy foliage has large, single yellow flowers. You may need to pin down canes to achieve low cover. Stout, sharp thorns make it a useful barrier.

Rubus calycinoides

'Nozomi'. A climbing miniature rose with trailing growth and small, glossy leaves, plant presents single, light pink flowers in clusters.

'Ralph's Creeper'. Light-centered, nearly single, 2-inch, bright red blossoms fade to pink. Spreading, moderate-size plant has matte green foliage.

'Rote Max Graf'. Large, single flowers resemble a red version of 'Max Graf' (above). Moderate-size, spreading plant has small, leathery, matte-finish leaves.

'Sea Foam'. Small, glossy leaves cover a mounding, spreading plant that bears clusters of medium-size, very double blossoms of white to cream.

'Swany'. Very double, flat white flowers adorn a trailing, medium-size to large plant with glossy, bronze-tinted foliage.

'White Meidiland'. Clusters of very double white flowers shine against a backdrop of dark, glossy leaves on a medium-size, spreading plant.

R. banksiae; Zones 8–10. Once-blooming species features small, very double blossoms in earliest spring; white and yellow forms are sold. This plant grows very large and bears evergreen foliage with narrow leaflets on thornless stems. Pin canes to the ground to achieve a low cover.

R. wichuraiana. This naturally prostrate species bears very glossy foliage; single white flowers bloom only in late spring. Plant is wide spreading and will root along stems as it spreads. Old-rose specialists may offer hybrids (wichuraiana ramblers) that have double flowers in white and pink shades; the best are those with French names, which have disease-resistant foliage. Avoid mildew-prone 'Dorothy Perkins'.

ROSMARINUS OFFICINALIS

ROSEMARY
Pictured on page 72

Zones: 7–10 (West), 7–8 (East)
Type: Evergreen shrub
Exposure: Sun
Water: Moderate to little
Spacing: 2 feet

Culinary rosemary is a variable species; several of its selected forms make durable, dense, low-maintenance ground covers. All have narrow, almost needlelike, leaves of medium to dark green with gray undersides; leaves are pungently scented and slightly sticky to the touch.

Small blue flowers appear from fall into spring, with peak display varying according to the variety. Stems root as

Rosmarinus officinalis 'Prostratus'

they spread, so that one plant becomes a colony of many individual but interconnected plants.

'Prostratus' is the most widely sold variety. Growth hugs the ground at first, but secondary stems arch, curve, or twist, giving a tumbled appearance to a mass planting. Growth may reach 2 feet high, but it can be kept lower with selective pruning. Planted at the edge of a raised bed, stems will trail over the side in waterfall fashion. Light gray blue flowers appear in late winter or early spring.

A similar plant is 'Lockwood de Forest', distinguished by blue flowers and lighter, brighter green foliage. 'Collingwood Ingram' is noted for its bright, violet blue flowers in early spring; plants grow 2 to 3 feet high, with stems curving outward and upward. 'Huntington Carpet' is the lowest growing of all, to 1½ feet high; its late winter flowers are an intense, bright blue.

Rosemary grows best in well-drained (even poor) soil; if not overwatered, it will prosper in heavier soils as well.

Water plants moderately during the first year until they become established; thereafter, water needs are minimal.

In cool-summer gardens, plants will remain attractive throughout the year with little or no supplemental water. In hot-summer regions, water rosemary occasionally in summer to keep plants looking fresh. In the desert, plants need periodic summer watering to survive.

RUBUS CALYCINOIDES

Pictured on page 71

Zones: 7–9
Type: Evergreen shrub
Exposure: Sun to light shade
Water: Moderate
Spacing: 2 feet

This blackberry relative boasts handsome foliage instead of tasty fruits. Individual leaves are round in general outline, 1 to 1½ inches across, with three to five broad lobes and ruffled margins. The lustrous, dark green upper surface has a rough texture; the gray white underside is feltlike.

Foliage covers the creeping, thornless stems, which spread at a moderate rate to make a dense cover to about a foot high. Hidden in the foliage are small white flowers that resemble strawberry blossoms. Nurseries may offer the superior selection 'Emerald Carpet'.

Give plants well-drained soil. They'll take light shade in all regions and will also thrive in full sun where summers are relatively cool.

SAGINA SUBULATA

IRISH MOSS, SCOTCH MOSS
Pictured on page 14

Zones: 5–10 (except intermediate and low desert)
Type: Evergreen perennial
Exposure: Sun to partial shade
Water: Regular watering
Spacing: 6 inches

Especially favored for planting among paving stones and rocks, these "mosses" can also be used to cover small areas in a green, velvetlike carpet.

Actually, there are two plants, *Arenaria verna* and *Sagina subulata,* so similar that they're interchangeable in the garden. (*Arenaria* has tiny white flowers

in clusters; blossoms of *Sagina* appear singly.) Green forms of both are sold as Irish moss; each also has a yellowish green variety 'Aurea' that may be sold as Scotch moss.

Choose good, well-drained soil for Irish and Scotch mosses. Plants are usually sold in flats. Cut squares from the flat and plant them so that the edges of the squares are at the same level or slightly lower than the soil surface; this helps prevent lumpiness.

In time, plantings will form humps; when this happens, cut out narrow strips and press the remaining turf into the soil.

SANTOLINA

Pictured on facing page

Zones: 7–10 (West), 7–8 (East)
Type: Evergreen shrub
Exposure: Sun
Water: Moderate to little
Spacing: 3 feet

Adaptability is a trait shared by both *Santolina* species described below. They grow easily in climates ranging from cool and dry to hot and moist. Established plants are quite tolerant of drought but will accept regular watering as long as the soil is reasonably well drained.

Left alone, a plant will spread widely; its many stems send up branches that arch upward to produce a billowy effect. But plants can be clipped or sheared to an even surface; one species, *S. chamaecyparissus,* is often grown as an ankle-height clipped hedge in formal herb plantings.

More common of the two species is lavender cotton, *S. chamaecyparissus,* with gray white foliage. Each leaf is very narrow and about an inch long; its margin is finely divided into feathery segments. Buttonlike, ½-inch yellow flowers (like daisies without petals) cover unsheared plants in late spring.

In contrast, *S. virens* has needlelike, bright green leaves about twice as long as lavender cotton's; its buttonlike flowers are creamy chartreuse.

In both species, foliage is pleasantly aromatic.

Without shearing or trimming, plants may grow 2 feet high. If older plantings become shabby, showing bare patches, cut back or shear plants heavily in early spring; dense new growth will fill in soon. For neatest appearance, shear off spent flowers after the flowering period.

SARCOCOCCA HOOKERANA HUMILIS

Zones: 6–10 (except desert)
Type: Evergreen shrub
Exposure: Shade to partial shade
Water: Regular watering
Spacing: 2 to 3 feet

Although this boxwood relative looks quite different, it shares boxwood's qualities of neatness and polish. Narrow, pointed-oval leaves are very dark green and glossy; they grow 3 inches long, closely set on the branches.

Plants may reach 1½ feet high and spread at a fairly slow rate by underground runners to 8 or more feet. Hidden among the leaves in winter or early spring are tiny, highly fragrant white flowers; these are followed by glossy, blue black fruits.

Best growth is in good soil liberally amended with organic matter. Plants prosper in shade everywhere, but they'll take sun where summer weather is cool and moist.

SAXIFRAGA STOLONIFERA

STRAWBERRY GERANIUM

Zones: 9–10 (except desert)
Type: Evergreen perennial
Exposure: Shade or partial shade
Water: Regular watering
Spacing: 12 to 18 inches

The common name of this ground cover comes both from the leaves, which resemble those of some true *Geranium* species, and from the plant's habit of spreading rapidly, in strawberry fashion, by long runners.

Fleshy leaves are nearly round, to 4 inches across, attractively veined in white with contrasting pink undersides. Foliage mass may reach 6 inches high. In spring,

slender stems grow to 2 feet and bear loose clusters of small white flowers.

Although plants should be watered regularly, they also need soil that drains well so that the roots won't rot.

Use this fine, small-scale ground cover with azaleas, rhododendrons, and other plants with similar moisture and drainage requirements.

SCAEVOLA 'MAUVE CLUSTERS'

Zones: 9–10 (West, except desert)
Type: Evergreen shrubby perennial
Exposure: Sun
Water: Moderate
Spacing: 3 feet

Where frost is rare or light, 'Mauve Clusters' excels as a trouble-free and nearly everblooming low ground cover. Spreading stems are densely clothed with oval, dark green leaves ¼ to ½ inch long; foliage mass may reach 6 inches high.

Sprinkled over the foliage are small clusters of ½-inch, bluish lilac flowers, each in an unusual fan or semicircular shape; plants flower nearly year-round in milder areas.

Once established, plants perform well in ordinary soil with infrequent watering. To enhance flower color, fertilize with iron sulfate.

SEDUM

STONECROP
Pictured on pages 15 and 74

Zones: Vary
Type: Evergreen succulent perennials
Exposure: Sun to partial shade
Water: Moderate
Spacing: 12 inches

Here are some of the best low-growing stonecrops, selected from the many species of *Sedum,* for use as ground covers. Foliage size, shape, and color vary, but all have thick, succulent leaves that are easily crushed.

Clustered small flowers, shaped like stars, are quite showy in some cases. All thrive in ordinary soil with no special care. New plants are easy to start from stem cuttings or from detached leaves.

Five stonecrops are cold tolerant enough to be grown in Zones 4–10. Goldmoss sedum, *S. acre,* has tiny, mosslike,

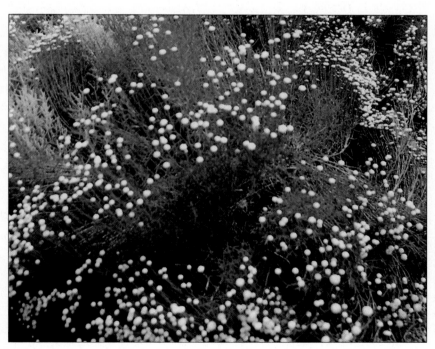
Santolina virens

light green leaves; yellow flowers bloom in late spring. Trailing stems send up branchlets 2 to 5 inches tall. Use gold-moss sedum to fill in between paving stones, among rocks, or as small-scale cover.

Equally low-growing *S. album* has nearly cylindrical, ½-inch leaves that are sometimes tinted red. Clusters of white to pinkish white flowers appear above the foliage in early summer.

For mosslike, dark green foliage, choose *S. anglicum;* spring flowers are pinkish white.

A larger plant, *S. lineare* (often sold as *S. sarmentosum*) grows to a foot high, bearing inch-long, narrow, light green leaves ('Variegatum' has leaves edged in white). Clusters of yellow flowers appear in late spring and early summer.

The thick, rounded leaves of *S. spurium* are an inch long and nearly as wide, carried in loose rosettes on trailing stems. Dense clusters of showy pink flowers appear in late summer. Popular variety 'Dragon's Blood' features bronze foliage and rose red flowers.

Several additional stonecrops are useful in warm areas of Zones 9–10.

Mexican sedum, *S. confusum* (often sold as *S. amecamecanum*), forms spreading clumps of upright stems 6 to 12 inches high. Rubbery, tongue-shaped leaves to 1½ inches long are bright, light green; leaves cluster in rosettes toward stem ends. Spring flowers are yellow, growing in dense clusters.

Mediterranean native *S. sediforme* (often sold as *S. altissimum*) has narrow, thick, blue gray leaves to 1½ inches long, closely set on stems that may reach 16 inches high. Summer flowers are greenish white.

A similar plant is *S. reflexum,* but its leaves are only ½ inch long and its blossoms are yellow.

Popular pork and beans, *S. rubro-tinctum,* has cylindrical, nearly inch-long leaves packed tightly on sprawling stems to make a cover 6 to 8 inches high. Each green leaf is tipped in reddish brown; the foliage may be totally bronze red in full sun. Spring flowers are yellow tinted with red.

SOLEIROLIA SOLEIROLII

BABY'S TEARS, ANGEL'S TEARS

Zones: 9–10
Type: Evergreen perennial
Exposure: Shade
Water: Regular watering
Spacing: 12 inches

Countless tiny, emerald green leaves on threadlike, interlacing stems create an undulating carpet that looks both cool and soft.

Baby's tears grows to 4 inches high in the shadiest locations, but it will remain lower in light or partial shade. Its tiny flowers are inconspicuous. Nurseries sometimes offer a variety with chartreuse gold foliage.

Under favorable shade and moisture conditions, baby's tears spreads quickly; it can become invasive, because even small pieces of stems will take root wherever they touch soil. Juicy leaves and stems are easily injured by foot traffic, but fast growth soon repairs any damage. Hard frosts turn plants into a black mush, but the onset of warmer weather initiates regrowth from the roots.

STACHYS BYZANTINA

LAMB'S EARS
Pictured on facing page

Zones: 4–10
Type: Evergreen to deciduous perennial
Exposure: Sun
Water: Moderate
Spacing: 18 inches

It's hard to resist touching the furry-surfaced, gray white leaves of lamb's ears. Thick, pointed-oval leaves reach 4 to 6 inches long, forming a solid cover of foliage from creeping stems that root as they spread.

Plants maintain an even cover about 8 inches high except in early summer, when branched 12- to 18-inch flower

Sedum spurium

stalks bear small, pinkish purple flowers in tiered whorls. Specialty nurseries may offer 'Silver Carpet', a form that produces no flowering stems.

Lamb's ears is undemanding, requiring only well-drained soil, but it's best used as a small-scale cover because it needs periodic grooming. Subfreezing weather will damage or kill the foliage; if this occurs, remove dead foliage in late winter or early spring before new growth starts.

After flowering ceases, cut out the flower stalks to restore neatness. (This also prevents the formation of seed, which can self-sow prolifically.) When bare patches begin to appear after several years, dig and divide plants; replant well-rooted divisions.

TAXUS BACCATA 'REPANDENS'

SPREADING ENGLISH YEW

Zones: 6–10 (except desert)
Type: Evergreen shrub
Exposure: Sun to shade
Water: Regular to moderate
Spacing: 3 feet

Spreading English yew, although botanically related to the familiar junipers (see page 57), produces a softer foliage effect in the landscape. Leaves are needlelike, about ½ inch long, and are borne in featherlike fashion on opposite sides of branches.

Growth is rather slow. Horizontal stems spread widely, forming a solid cover in time. You can keep it low—to several inches high—by shearing or clipping, or you can allow branches to build up to around 2 feet. Foliage color is rich green, but the variety 'Repandens Aurea' produces golden yellow new growth.

In fall, small, berrylike red fruits form on the branches if there's a pistillate (male) English yew planted nearby.

Plants prosper in soils ranging from acid to slightly alkaline, as long as the soil

Stachys byzantina

drains well. Growth is equally good in sun or shade, even dense shade beneath trees. Avoid planting against south- or west-facing walls where the foliage can burn from reflected heat and light.

TEUCRIUM CHAMAEDRYS

GERMANDER
Pictured on page 76

Zones: 6–10 (West), 6–7 (East)
Type: Evergreen shrubby perennial
Exposure: Sun to partial shade
Water: Moderate to little
Spacing: 18 to 24 inches

Trouble-free germander consistently provides a dark green carpet, even when soil is poor or watering is infrequent. Plants have many spreading stems and ascending branches that rise to about 12 inches; stems bear oval leaves nearly an inch long with prominently toothed edges. Variety 'Prostratum' grows only 4 to 6 inches high, spreading widely.

In summer, loose spikes of small, pinkish purple or white flowers appear at stem ends.

Germander isn't fussy about soil quality, but too much moisture is an enemy. Plants grown in well-drained soil will take regular to little watering; in heavy, clay-like soil, water infrequently. If plants become straggly, shear back to encourage lower, branching growth.

Teucrium chamaedrys

THYMUS

THYME

Zones: 4–10
Type: Evergreen perennials
Exposure: Sun to light shade
Water: Moderate
Spacing: 12 inches

Several of the aromatic thymes can provide attractive cover between paving stones and in small patches in rock gardens. These include caraway-scented thyme, *T. herba-barona,* and furry, gray-leafed woolly thyme, *T. pseudolanuginosus.*

For larger expanses, the best choice is *T. praecox arcticus* (sometimes sold as *T. serpyllum* or *T. drucei*), popularly called creeping thyme or mother-of-thyme. Its initial stems form a flat mat; above it rise upright branches 2 to 6 inches high bearing tiny, rounded, pleasantly pungent leaves. In late spring and early summer, rounded clusters of small, lilac purple flowers blossom at branch tips. Some nurseries also offer 'Reiter's', which has rosy red blossoms, as well as a white-flowered variety.

All thymes prefer well-drained, nutrient-poor soil that's fairly dry. In hot-summer regions, however, plants need periodic watering during the warmest months. If a planting becomes straggly, you can shear or cut back stems.

TRACHELOSPERMUM JASMINOIDES

STAR JASMINE, CONFEDERATE JASMINE
Pictured on facing page

Zones: 9–10
Type: Evergreen vine
Exposure: Sun to partial shade
Water: Regular watering
Spacing: 3 feet

Although not a true jasmine, star jasmine possesses a similar and equally penetrating perfume.

The handsome plant is a twining vine that, when unsupported, will cover the ground at a moderate rate, building to a depth of about 2 feet. When star jasmine is grown in a raised bed or on a retained hillside, its stems will spill gracefully over the side of the confining wall.

Leathery, glossy leaves are pointed ovals to 3 inches long, maturing from light green new growth to dark green foliage. Against this polished backdrop, clusters of 1-inch, pinwheel-shaped white flowers bloom in summer (late spring in the desert); their intense fragrance carries for some distance.

A similar species is *T. asiaticum;* its leaves are smaller and less glossy, and flowers range from yellow to cream in color.

Star jasmine thrives in average, well-drained soil; where summer is especially hot, and certainly in the desert, locate plants in partial shade. Fertilize at the start of the growing season and again after flowering to encourage lush growth. Chlorosis may develop in alkaline soil; if this occurs, treat with iron chelate or iron sulfate.

VANCOUVERIA PLANIPETALA

INSIDE-OUT FLOWER

Zones: 7–9 (except desert)
Type: Evergreen perennial
Exposure: Shade
Water: Regular to moderate
Spacing: 12 to 18 inches

The curious common name refers to the odd shape of this plant's flower, which looks as though its petals had been swept back in a strong wind. A lesser-known name, redwood ivy, aptly describes its foliage. Individual leaflets resemble shallowly lobed ivy leaves carried on wirelike leaf stalks that grow from a thick mat of creeping underground stems. This carpet of overlapping foliage may reach as high as 2 feet.

In late spring, large, open flower clusters rise above the foliage on slender stems, each cluster comprised of 25 to 50 individual white blossoms less than ½ inch across.

Nurseries specializing in western native plants may carry other *Vancouveria* species that will be equally useful in shaded gardens.

VERBENA

Zones: Vary (West only)
Type: Evergreen perennial
Exposure: Sun
Water: Moderate
Spacing: 12 to 18 inches

Few ground covers surpass the verbenas for amount of color provided over an extended period of time. Flat-topped clusters of brightly colored small flowers nearly hide the foliage at the peak of summer bloom.

These low, spreading plants grow rapidly in sunny situations from coast to desert; hot summer weather actually encourages top performance. Plants are not particular about soil and need only moderate watering. In late winter or early spring, shear or cut back established plantings; then apply fertilizer.

Most verbenas are rather short-lived perennials; you may need to replace them after several years.

The basic type of ground-hugging *V. peruviana* (Zones 9–10) offers vivid scarlet flowers on a vigorous plant with small, oval leaves. Nurseries also carry numerous hybrid varieties—some sold by name, others labeled only by color—that have slightly larger foliage and grow to about 12 inches high. In addition to red, available colors include pink, magenta, purple, blue, and white.

Garden verbena, *V. hybrida* (Zones 9–10), is often planted as an annual but will persist for several years. Spreading plants grow 6 to 12 inches high and are clothed in oblong green or gray green leaves 2 to 4 inches long. Colors are the same as listed for *V. peruviana*, above; named strains are available. Plants are somewhat subject to mildew; to minimize the problem, water deeply and infrequently.

Two verbenas native to the Southwest make effective ground covers in Zones 5–10. Plants of *V. bipinnatifida* grow 8 to 15 inches high, bearing very finely divided leaves and clusters of blue flowers. Reaching several inches taller, *V. goodingii* features pinkish lavender flowers above deeply cut foliage. Both species perpetuate themselves in the garden by reseeding.

VERONICA

SPEEDWELL

Zones: 6–10
Type: Evergreen to deciduous perennials
Exposure: Sun to partial shade
Water: Regular watering
Spacing: 12 inches

The speedwells form low carpets of small, pointed leaves from which rise upright spikes or small clusters of sparkling blue or white flowers. Use these plants in small areas (they'll provide good cover for spring-flowering bulbs) and between paving stones.

Creeping speedwell, *V. repens*, forms a low mat of shiny foliage. Plants are evergreen in Zones 9–10; in colder areas, they lose their leaves in fall and regrow them in spring. Small clusters of ¼-inch lavender or white flowers appear in spring.

A slightly larger, higher plant, *V. prostrata* (*V. rupestris*) has mintlike leaves to 1½ inches long. Light blue flowers cluster atop 8-inch stems; lower-growing 'Heavenly Blue' has flowers of a darker, more intense shade.

Trachelospermum jasminoides

VIBURNUM DAVIDII

Zones: 7–10 (except desert)
Type: Evergreen shrub
Exposure: Shade to partial shade
Water: Regular to moderate
Spacing: 18 inches

Although springtime brings small clusters of white flowers, it's the foliage that makes this viburnum a garden ornament. Pointed-oval leaves may reach 6 inches long; they're dark green and glossy, with prominent veins that run from base to tip.

Plants spread slowly to form small clumps 1 to 2 feet high; the elegant foliage makes a solid cover. In a mass planting, attractive metallic blue fruits will form after the flowers fade.

Best-looking foliage comes on plants grown in good soil and watered regularly, although plants in cool climates or heavy soil may thrive with moderate watering. Control height by cutting back any stems that grow too tall.

VINCA

PERIWINKLE, MYRTLE
Pictured below

Zones: Vary
Type: Evergreen perennials
Exposure: Sun to shade
Water: Moderate
Spacing: 18 inches

Ease of growth and general attractiveness are assets of both *Vinca* species; the drawback is potential invasiveness—particularly in shade and with *V. major*.

Plants send out spreading or arching green stems bearing pairs of shiny, oval leaves. Stems may root at the joints or even at the tips when they touch moist soil; each newly rooted part is then capable of sending out additional stems. Flowers that resemble single phlox blossoms appear in spring.

Plants are undemanding and willing to grow in any soil; they even compete well with surface tree roots. In cool-

Vinca minor

summer regions, the periwinkles can take full sun as well as shade; where summers are hot, partial shade to shade produces the best appearance.

If plantings mound up too high or become too layered with old stems, shear or mow them in late winter to bring on new growth close to the ground.

V. major (Zones 8–10), the larger of the two species, has broadly oval leaves to 3 inches on stems that may build up a planting to about 2 feet high. Lavender blue (often called periwinkle blue) flowers, 1 to 2 inches across, are scattered over the foliage. To enliven shaded plantings, use the variety with creamy white variegated leaves.

Dwarf periwinkle, *V. minor* (Zones 4–10), resembles a miniature version of *V. major*. However, growth is lower and more prostrate, and the narrower leaves are spaced more closely on the stems. Flowers are an inch across, their greater abundance making a showier display than *V. major*.

Available varieties have flowers of white and various shades of blue; some even have double blossoms. You'll also find a form with variegated leaves.

VIOLA

Violet
Pictured on facing page and page 13

Zones: Vary
Type: Evergreen, deciduous perennials
Exposure: Sun to shade
Water: Regular watering
Spacing: 12 inches

The fragrant purple violets used in a romantic nosegay are just one of several different violets available for ground cover use. All have rounded leaves, borne at the ends of slender leaf stalks, that make solid, low carpets of foliage. Flowers rise in great profusion just above the foliage mass.

For best growth, plant in good soil and water regularly. Apply fertilizer in early spring to enhance bloom production and general appearance. Where summers are cool, violets can grow in sun, but in hot-summer regions they need at least afternoon shade.

Evergreen sweet violet, *V. odorata* (Zones 6–10), is the beloved fragrant species; it begins to bloom in late winter or early spring, depending on winter cold. Purple is considered the traditional color, but specialists carry many named varieties with flowers of blue, lavender, violet, pink, or white. Plants spread in strawberry fashion, forming new plants at the ends of runners.

Deciduous Confederate violet, *V. sororia* (sometimes sold as *V. priceana*), grows in Zones 6–10; it forms clumps of thick rootstocks. Unless spent flowers are removed, plantings will self-seed profusely. Spring flowers resemble small pansies in white, heavily veined with blue.

Australian violet, *V. hederacea*, thrives in Zones 8–10 (except desert). When temperatures drop to 30°F/-1°C, the plant goes deciduous. Late spring to summer flowers are blue or violet, broadly edged in white; the effect is of white flowers with a dark central patch. Plants spread slowly by stolons.

Viola hederacea

WALDSTEINIA FRAGARIOIDES

BARREN STRAWBERRY

Zones: 5–10 (except desert)
Type: Evergreen perennial
Exposure: Sun to light shade
Water: Regular watering
Spacing: 12 inches

One of three strawberry like ground covers (see also *Duchesnea indica,* page 45, and *Fragaria chiloensis,* page 47), this plant also forms a thick carpet of strawberry-lookalike leaves 2 to 3 inches high. But this plant spreads more slowly than the other two and is less likely to overgrow its confines.

Small clusters of ¾-inch, single yellow flowers appear in spring but form no fruits. Fall brings another show of color when the glossy green leaves turn to bronzy red.

WEDELIA TRILOBATA

WEDELIA

Zones: 9 (warmest parts)–10
Type: Evergreen perennial
Exposure: Sun to shade
Water: Regular watering
Spacing: 18 inches

Within the limits of its cold tolerance, wedelia is remarkably adaptable, growing well at the seashore and in the low desert. Basic needs are only well-drained soil and regular moisture. Frost will kill wedelia to the ground, but if freezes are not sustained, the plant will regrow quickly with the onset of warmer weather.

Glossy, fleshy leaves to 4 inches long make a thick, lush carpet; for most of the year, it's decorated with inch-wide yellow flowers that resemble single marigolds. Plants spread rapidly and extensively by creeping stems that root as they spread. When older plantings become too thick or uneven, shear or cut them back heavily.

ZOYSIA TENUIFOLIA

KOREAN GRASS

Zones: 9–10
Type: Evergreen perennial grass
Exposure: Sun to light shade
Water: Moderate
Spacing: 8 to 12 inches

An established planting of Korean grass resembles a piece of rumpled velour. Tiny blades of rich green are densely packed into a mounding, undulating turf that never needs mowing and will accept some foot traffic. You can use it in moderately large expanses or in small spaces; between paving stones it forms a velvety green "mortar."

Korean grass prefers well-drained soil but will grow in claylike soil if not overwatered. Leaf blades turn brown with the first frost; they'll return to green at the onset of warm weather in spring.

Index